SELF ASSESSMENT
FOR THE Small Business
AND THE Self-Employed

Self Assessment
for the Small Business
and the Self-Employed

a step-by-step guide

Niki Chesworth

THE EXPRESS

YOURS TO HAVE AND TO HOLD
BUT NOT TO COPY

The publication you are reading is protected by copyright law. This means that the publisher could take you and your employer to court and claim heavy legal damages if you make unauthorised photocopies from these pages. Photocopying copyright material without permission is no different from stealing a magazine from a newsagent, only it doesn't seem like theft.

The Copyright Licensing Agency (CLA) is an organisation which issues licences to bring photocopying within the law. It has designed licensing services to cover all kinds of special needs in business, education and government.

If you take photocopies from books, magazines and periodicals at work your employer should be licensed with CLA. Make sure you are protected by a photocopying licence.

The Copyright Licensing Agency Limited, 90 Tottenham Court Road, London, W1P 0LP. Tel: 0171 436 5931. Fax: 0171 436 3986.

First published in 1998

Apart from any fair dealing for the purposes of research or private study, or criticism or review, as permitted under the Copyright, Designs and Patents Act 1988, this publication may only be reproduced, stored or transmitted, in any form or by any means, with the prior permission in writing of the publishers, or in the case of reprographic reproduction in accordance with the terms and licences issued by the CLA. Enquiries concerning reproduction outside those terms should be sent to the publishers at the undermentioned address:

Kogan Page Limited
120 Pentonville Road
London N1 9JN

© Niki Chesworth, 1998

British Library Cataloguing in Publication Data
A CIP record for this book is available from the British Library.
ISBN 0 7494 2679 9

Typeset by FSH.
Printed and bound in Great Britain by Clays Ltd, St Ives plc

CONTENTS

Introduction		vii

Part 1: How Small and Medium-Sized Businesses Are Taxed

1	A Basic Course in Income Tax	3
2	A Basic Course in Capital Gains Tax	12
3	A Basic Guide to National Insurance Contributions	27
4	A Basic Guide to VAT	35
5	Accounts and Tax	46
6	Employing Staff	52
7	Dealing with the Inland Revenue and Customs	56

Part 2: Ways To Save Tax

8	Making Sure You Claim the Maximum Expenses	65
9	Deducting Capital Expenses	76

Part 3: Filling in Your Tax Return

10	The Questionnaire	85
11	Self-Employment	90
12	Partnerships	105
13	Savings Interest and Share Dividends	107

14 Pensions, Social Security Benefits, Maintenance Payments and Other Income	116
15 Tax Relief on Pensions, Mortgages, Charitable Giving and Other Loans and Investments	132
16 Tax Allowances	149
17 Tax Refunds, Calculations and Other Information	162
18 Calculating Your Tax Bill	170
19 A Guide to the Other Supplementary Pages	172

INTRODUCTION

It is hard to find time to think about tax when you are spending every hour possible trying to run a business. In fact, as most readers of this book will probably agree, it is hard to think about tax even if you have the time.

But it is essential that you understand how taxation works, how it affects every business decision you make and what you must do to comply with tax laws so you do not face fines – or worse, the closure of your business.

Tax savings can be made nearly every time you make a purchase or plan ahead. Should you buy or lease your equipment? Should you buy an asset now or wait until the next tax year? Should you set up a pension scheme to save tax? You can only know the answers to these questions if you know the tax implications.

Most of the self-employed employ an accountant to prepare their accounts and file their tax returns. But many do not realize the need for – or cannot afford – more sophisticated tax and accountancy advice.

This book gives you this advice, in the simplest terms possible and with the minimum of jargon.

It is packed full of tax-saving tips which should mean that every reader saves far, far more than the cost of this book.

PART 1:
HOW SMALL AND MEDIUM-SIZED BUSINESSES ARE TAXED

This book looks at the taxation of the self-employed, known as Schedule D I income tax (and the case of partners as Schedule D II). Limited companies are taxed differently under Corporation Tax.

1

A BASIC COURSE IN INCOME TAX

The self-employed are taxed on the total of their business profits and other personal income. This means that your profits from self-employment are added to your savings, investment, rental and other income as well as any capital gains before calculating the amount of tax you need to pay.

So, in addition to knowing how business profits are calculated and taxed, the self-employed must also understand how all other types of income are taxed. As such this chapter looks at both business and personal taxation.

Capital Gains Tax, the tax on profits from the sale of shares, investments and other assets including business assets is covered in Chapter 2. The other 'tax' assessed using the Tax Return is **Class 4 National Insurance if you are self-employed**. This is covered in Chapter 3.

Note: This book looks at the rates in the tax year 6 April 1997 to 5 April 1998 – the year covered by the Tax Return sent out in April 1998.

TAX-FREE INCOME

Some types of income are tax-free and **you do not have to include these on your Tax Return**. These include:

- income from National Savings Certificates;
- the first £70 of interest from National Savings Bank ordinary accounts;
- premium bond prizes;
- proceeds from most life insurance policies;
- income from Personal Equity Plans (PEPs) – however, these will

HOW SMALL AND MEDIUM-SIZED BUSINESSES ARE TAXED

be replaced from April 1999 by the new Individual Savings Account;
- maintenance payments paid by your former spouse or the father of your children to set up limits and subject to certain conditions;
- some employee benefits such as a subsidized canteen, profit-related pay for employees and the first £30,000 of redundancy for employees;
- some social security benefits including:
  – child benefit (although this may change) and allowances;
  – housing benefits;
  – maternity allowance;
  – sickness benefit;
  – family credit;
  – income support (in most cases).
  (**Note**: The government plans to integrate the tax and benefits systems so the tax situation of certain benefits could change.)

And the following do not count as income and so are not taxed:

- prizes and betting winnings including the lottery, competitions and gambling;
- gifts and presents (but not if they are for work done).

Note: If you sell an asset (but not trading stock) this does not get taxed as income but may be liable for Capital Gains Tax – the tax you pay on the profit you make when you sell an asset such as shares, investments, second homes and businesses.

If you inherit money or assets these are taxed under Inheritance Tax before you receive them, if the estate exceeds the tax threshold. However, if interest was earned on the estate (the amount of wealth and assets left by someone when they die) while that estate was being administered, you may have to pay tax on that income.

INCOME TAX RATES AND TAX BANDS

Income Tax for the 1997/98 tax year was charged at three different *tax rates* on income that falls into different tax bands. You only pay each rate of Income Tax on income that falls within a tax band of earnings. This means that you can pay tax at the lower rate, basic rate and higher rate if you have income in each of these tax bands.

The amount of tax charged on each tax band has been calculated for you in Table 1.1.

Table 1.1 *Income Tax: The Different Tax Rates and Tax Bands*

Tax rate	%	Income Tax band Tax year 1997/98	Tax you will have to pay
Lower	20%	The first **£4100** of taxable income in excess of your allowances	(20% of £4100) **£820**
Basic	23%	The next **£4101** to **£26,100** of taxable income (£22,000 of income)	23% of £22,000 **£5060**
Higher	40%	Taxable income in excess of **£26,100**	40% of income above this limit

These income bands are in addition to your tax allowance – so you only pay tax on income above your allowance. The income covered by your allowance is tax-free regardless of your rate of tax.

TAX ALLOWANCES

You do not have to pay tax on all of your income. You are entitled to what is called a *tax allowance* – the amount you can earn **before** you have to pay tax.

The main allowances you will receive automatically or can claim are:

- **Personal allowance.** Everyone has a Personal allowance, but you are only allowed one. If you have more than one job or are an employee and self-employed, you may find that the personal allowance is used to reduce the tax you pay on your wages as it will be included in your Tax Code.
- **Married couple's allowance.** This is in addition to your personal allowance and is given if you are married. If you wed part way through the tax year your allowance will be reduced proportionately. The allowance is given to the husband. The wife can claim half without her husband's consent and all of it with his agreement.
- **Age allowances.** The personal allowance rises with age. To qualify for an age allowance you must have reached 65 by the end of the tax year, 5 April 1998. A higher allowance is given to those aged 75 and over. The married couple's age allowance is also increased if either of the couple is aged 65 or over at the end of the tax year.

HOW SMALL AND MEDIUM-SIZED BUSINESSES ARE TAXED

☐ **Single parent allowance**. This is officially called the 'additional personal allowance'. It is given to those who have a child living with them and who are single, divorced or widowed.

How allowances reduce your tax bill

Your tax allowance is how much you can earn **before** paying tax, **not** the amount of tax you save. How much tax you save depends on your top rate of tax.

The personal tax allowance means that you do not have to pay tax on £4045 of taxable income in the April 1997 to April 1998 tax year. So you save the tax you would have had to pay on that proportion of your income.

If you would normally pay 23 per cent tax on that income you save:

23% of £4045 = **£930**

However, if you are a higher rate taxpayer and pay 40 per cent tax on your highest earnings, your savings will be as follows:

40% of £4045 = **£1618**

But you can only save 40 per cent tax on income taxed at 40 per cent. So, if you only have £1000 of earnings taxed in the higher-rate tax bracket, you will only save 40 per cent on the £1000. Your savings on the remaining allowance of £3045 will be at the basic-tax rate of 23 per cent.

Some allowances have *relief restrictions*, which means that the rate of tax relief is restricted to a certain rate of tax as in the case of the *married couple's allowance*. This means that instead of saving up to 40 per cent of the allowance you can only save 15 per cent.

So the tax savings are as follows for **both** basic-rate and higher-rate taxpayers:

15% of £1830 = **£274.50**

Special rules for pensioners

The age allowance given to those aged 65 and over has an *earnings restriction*. This means that if you had a total taxable income of more than £15,600 in the April 1997 to April 1998 tax year your allowances would be reduced by £1 for every £2 you earned over this limit. The allowance only stops being reduced when it is cut to the basic personal allowance of £4045. So the more you earn the less tax savings you make. If your basic allowance is cut to £4045 and you have not deducted all your earnings deduction, your higher age-related married couple's allowances will then be reduced. But once again it cannot be reduced to below the basic allowance of £1830.

For a full listing of tax allowances and the resultant tax savings, see Table 1.2.

Table 1.2 *Tax allowances for the April 1997 – April 1998 tax year*

Type of allowance	1997/98 allowance	Amount of tax saving for basic rate taxpayer and rate at which tax savings are made	Amount of tax saving for higher rate taxpayer and and rate at which tax savings are made
Standard personal allowance	£4045	£930 (at 23%)	£1618 (at 40%)
Standard married couples allowance*	£1830	£275 (at 15%)	£275 (at 15%)
Aged 65 to 74: Personal allowance	£5220	£1201 (at 23%)	£2088 (at 40%)
Aged 65 to 74: Married couples allowance*	£3185	£733 (at 15%)	£733 (at 15%)
Aged 75 and over personal allowance	£5400	£1242 (at 23%)	£2160 (at 40%)
Aged 75 and over married couples allowance*	£3225	£484 (at 15%)	£484 (at 15%)
Additional personal allowance for single parents*	£1830	£275 (at 15%)	£275 (at 15%)
Widows bereavement allowance*	£1830	£275 (at 15%)	£275 (at 15%)
Blind person allowance	£1280	£294 (at 23%)	£512 (at 40%)
Income limit for age-related allowances**	£15,600		

*   Relief restricted to 15 per cent – this means that regardless of the tax rate you pay you can only get a tax saving at 15 per cent. This is to restrict the tax advantage and to make it the same for all taxpayers.

** Age allowances reduced by £1 for every £2 income in excess of the limit until the basic non-age-related allowance is reached – so if you earn £1000 over the limit your higher age-related personal allowance will be reduced by £500.

TAX CODES

The self-employed are not given Tax Codes, but they are covered in this book for those who:

- are also employees;
- who receive company pensions; and/or
- are employers themselves and therefore need to understand the Tax Codes of their employees.

Tax Codes are given to those who receive income under PAYE (Pay-As-You-Earn), the system for collecting taxes from wages and salaries and company pensions. The code adjusts an individual's *tax allowances* so a greater or lesser amount of tax can be deducted from his or her salary or company pension before it is paid. This enables the Inland Revenue to collect any extra tax or give additional tax relief.

The code is made up of numbers (usually three) and a letter, for example:

312H or K311

The figures in the code show the amount you can earn in the tax year before paying tax. When working out your Tax Code the last number is deleted. So if the individual can earn £4045 before paying tax the code will be 404 (one-tenth of net allowances rounded down). The letter next to these numbers tells the employer the tax status of the individual.

The numbers

The Inland Revenue adds up all *allowances,* including the personal allowance and married couple's allowance, and may add on a sum to give the tax relief the employee is due for Personal Pension Plan contributions or maintenance payments. There may also be a sum for job expenses – this is to ensure that the employee is not taxed on expenses that are allowable and not taxable.

Then it adds up any *deductions* to tax employee perks and benefits-in-kind (such as company cars or private medical insurance) and other sources of income such as untaxed (gross) interest. The figures included for employee perks on the code are usually the *cash* equivalent values of your perks. This amount is usually the cost to your employer, although for company cars it is 35 per cent of the list price. You are taxed on these perks by an adjustment in your Tax Code. The Inland Revenue subtracts the amount of *deductions* from the amount of *allowances* and gets a final figure.

The letters

These tell the employer how to treat the Tax Code by breaking down employees into different types of taxpayer. This is what the most commonly used letters mean. The employee is entitled to:

- L The basic personal allowance.
- H The personal allowance and the married couple's allowance.
- P The higher age-related personal allowance for those aged between 65 and 74.
- K No tax free allowance at all because the value of any perks and other deductibles is greater than the allowances – see below.

Note if an employee has a 'T' code, tax is not adjusted by the employer but by the Tax Office.

The 'K' code

This means the individual has a negative allowance, ie deductions are greater than allowances. It not only means that **all** income is taxed (there is no tax-free allowance) but also that extra tax must be deducted from pay each pay day.

For example:

Mr K has total allowances of	£4045
His total deductions are	£5050
So he has a **negative** amount of allowance for the tax year of	= - £1005
His code will be 100K.	
The extra £1005 is added to his income. So, he is paid monthly: £1005 ÷12	= £84
So every month he will pay tax on **all** his salary plus tax on a further £84 will be deducted from his pay.	

HOW SMALL AND MEDIUM-SIZED BUSINESSES ARE TAXED

Note: More information on the taxation of employees is given in Chapter 6 on employing staff.

TAX RELIEF

Tax relief reduces your tax bill by refunding tax you have already paid or by reducing the amount of tax you are liable to pay. Sometimes tax relief is given automatically so you do not notice that you are getting a rebate. In other cases you have to claim the tax relief on your Tax Return.

For example, if you are a higher-rate taxpayer you will get tax relief of 40p for every £1 you put in your pension. But you can only get tax relief at 40 per cent if you pay tax at 40 per cent and you have to have enough higher-rate earnings to qualify.

So, if you want to claim tax relief at 40 per cent on £1000 invested in your pension but you only have £600 of earnings taxed at 40 per cent the Inland Revenue will only give you top rate tax relief on the £600. You will get basic-rate tax relief of 23 per cent on the remaining £400 you invest.

See Part 3 on filling in Your Tax Return for more information on how tax relief works, how much you can claim and how to claim.

There is also *reduced rate tax relief* which restricts the rate of tax relief – so if you pay tax at 40 per cent you may only be able to claim the tax relief at 15 per cent.

You don't always have to claim tax relief. Sometimes you get *tax relief at source*. Most mortgages come under MIRAS – *mortgage interest tax relief at source* – which means your mortgage lender will automatically give you tax relief on your mortgage payments up to the *tax relief limit* of £30,000 and will give you this tax relief at the correct reduced rate of 10 per cent from April 1998 (in the 1997-98 tax year the rate was 15 per cent). This tax relief means your mortgage payments are automatically reduced.

TAX AT SOURCE

Just as you can receive *tax relief at source*, you can also be taxed at source. This means that tax is already deducted before you receive your income.

This happens with employees whose tax is deducted under the PAYE (Pay-As-You-Earn) system using their Tax Code to work out how much of their earnings can be tax free.

Most bank and building society income is also taxed at source. Although tax is currently deducted at 20 per cent, only higher-rate taxpayers need to pay any additional tax. Basic, 23 per cent tax payers, do not need to pay any additional tax even though tax has been deducted at the lower rate.

The same applies to share dividends which are paid after 20 per cent tax has been deducted.

Non-taxpayers can currently reclaim the tax deducted or, in the case of savings accounts, ask their bank or building society to pay the interest gross (without tax deducted).

A BASIC COURSE IN CAPITAL GAINS TAX

In addition to Income Tax, Capital Gains Tax is the other major tax that is assessed through your Tax Return. These two taxes cover most of the money you are likely to receive – one taxes your income and the other your profits.

You pay Capital Gains Tax if you sell or *dispose* of an *asset* – a possession, investment or business – and you receive *capital* – a sum of cash – and have made a *gain*. You pay the tax on the gain you make, minus certain allowances, **not** on the amount you receive when you sell the asset.

There is a much higher allowance (the amount you can earn before tax) than for Income Tax. You are allowed to make profits of £6500 on gains in the 1997/98 tax year. Note this is for all assets sold – not per item. There are ways to avoid paying Capital Gains Tax and some items are exempt and as a result only 90,000 taxpayers actually pay the tax each year.

ASSETS LIABLE TO CAPITAL GAINS TAX

These include:

- businesses;
- shares;
- land (apart from the grounds of your home if they are fewer than one and a quarter acres);
- second homes;
- antiques and works of art;
- unit and investments trusts;
- jewellery and silver;

- and most things you hold for personal or investment purposes – basically any asset that is not exempt.

ASSETS EXEMPT FROM CAPITAL GAINS TAX

These include:

- private cars (unless you sell them for a business or regularly sell them at a profit);
- your main home (principal private residence) provided you have not let it out or used it for business;
- personal possessions or chattels, with a predicted useful life of 50 years or less when you got them;
- Personal Equity Plans (PEPs), bonuses from TESSA accounts, National Savings investments, gilts – UK government stocks and some corporate bonds bought after 13 March 1984;
- shares issued under the enterprise investment scheme and venture capital trusts;
- British money (including post-1837 gold sovereigns) and foreign currency for personal use;
- betting and lottery winnings;
- life insurance policies (with some exceptions – mainly short-term policies and those bought from a third party not the life insurance company);
- qualifying corporate bonds (but not on a company share reorganization or takeover);
- personal injury compensation;
- damages including those for defamation or personal injury;
- trading stock you sell (if you are running a business);
- inheritances – when you die there is no capital gains on your estate but Inheritance Tax may be charged. However, when you sell an inheritance you may be liable to Capital Gains Tax on any profits you have made while you have owned the inheritance.

Tax tips:

- Whenever possible you should try to use up your Capital Gains Tax allowance. You can do this by spreading the sale of assets over a number of years rather than selling them at the same time, so you do not make a massive profit in one year, or by using a tax avoidance system known as *bed and breakfasting* which enables you to sell shares, unit or

investment trusts at the end of the tax year to use up your Capital Gains Tax allowance and then buy the same assets back the next day. Your stockbroker, unit trust or investment trust company will tell you how to do this cheaply. You can also use this to make a deliberate loss. This loss can then reduce any gains you make in that year.
- To avoid the risk of having to pay Capital Gains Tax on the sale of shares invest using a Personal Equity Plan (PEP). You can invest up to £3000 a year in a single-share PEP and £6000 in a general PEP. But note that PEPs will be abolished from April 1999. You will be able to transfer PEP investments into their replacement, the Individual Savings Account.

HOW DO I KNOW IF I HAVE MADE A GAIN?

You may make a gain if an asset you have sold has risen in value since you bought it (or since 31 March 1982 if you bought the asset before then and want to use this date). You do not pay tax on the first £6500 of gains (this limit is for the sale of **all** assets) and you only pay tax on gains above this limit. You will pay Capital Gains Tax at your top rate of tax for the 1997/8 tax year.

Note
- The March 1998 Budget reduced the equivalent Capital Gains Tax rates for business assets. From April 1998 the rate will fall from 40 per cent to 10 per cent for higher-rate tax payers over the next 10 years, provided assets are held for ten years from 5 April 1998. So, the 10 per cent rate will not apply in 2008. Capital gains on non-business assets will reduce from 40 per cent for higher-rate tax payers to 24 per cent. Assets acquired before 17 March 1998 will qualify for an additional one year's ownership. The tapering of relief is given on assets held for a complete tax year – not a part year.

You may make a capital gain even if you do not sell an asset – for instance, if you give it away, exchange it or sell the rights to it or you get insurance money if it is lost or destroyed. If you do not sell the asset, the market value of the asset at the time of disposal is usually taken as its value when calculating Capital Gains Tax. The date you dispose of an asset is the date that you must use when calculating your profit, not necessarily the date you are paid.

And you can still make a chargeable gain (a profit liable to Capital Gains Tax) if you only sell part of an asset. You are also classed as making a gain if you receive another item in exchange or agree to be paid in future. If you only sell part of an asset (or retain an interest in part of an asset) you can only claim expenditure which relates wholly to the part disposed of or a proportion of expenditure which relates to the part sold. Ask for Inland Revenue *Help Sheet IR284* which covers shares and capital gains tax.

To work out if you have made a gain you must calculate the profit. Take the price you sold the asset for (or its market value on the date it was given as a gift, exchanged or lost) and deduct:

- the price you paid for the asset or its value at the time it was given to you;
- costs incurred in buying and selling – including valuer's/surveyor's fees, auction fees, the cost of legal advice, stamp duty, advertising costs, stockbroking fees;
- costs of enhancing the value of the asset – restoration etc;
- inflation – but only between 31 March 1982 and 1 April 1989 (see indexing allowance below).

You cannot deduct:

- interest you paid on a loan used to buy the asset.

If you held/owned the asset on **31 March 1982** you can elect to substitute its market value on that date instead of the actual original purchase cost. This is known as *rebasing*. So any appreciation/profit you made before that date will not be taxed. In this case you can substitute this 1982 market value for the original price you paid unless you are valuing shares, in which case the share value on 31 March 1982 applies. If you use a valuation include this on your Tax Return. If you are unsure what value to use ask your Tax Officer. The Inland Revenue uses its own specialist valuers and you will be able to discuss with them what value to use. If you rebase you **cannot** include any expenses incurred before 31 March 1982.

However, once you have elected for rebasing this will cover **all** your assets and you cannot change your mind. But if you have not made such an election you can treat each asset differently. As such, you can work out gains from the original purchase date if your gains will be lower.

In this case you can also claim expenses incurred before 31 March 1982. But indexation (the factor that adjusts your gain to take into account inflation) did not start until March 1982. So you can only deduct the effects of inflation from March 1982 onwards.

HOW SMALL AND MEDIUM-SIZED BUSINESSES ARE TAXED

In some cases one figure (say gains since 1982) will produce a loss and the other (gains since you purchased the item) a profit. In this case ask your Tax Officer for advice as you may not have to pay any Capital Gains Tax.

If you want **all** of your assets owned on 31 March 1982 rebased to that date, you must make a *rebasing election*. If you are planning to rebase your gains ask for Inland Revenue *Help Sheet IR280*. Remember, once you have decided to do this you cannot change your mind.

You can also deduct an *indexation allowance* from your gains in the 1997/98 tax year. This is an allowance for inflation. So if you only made a profit because inflation pushed up the value of your asset, you should not have to pay Capital Gains Tax. It works by comparing the Retail Price Index in the month you bought an asset and in the month when you sold it. For example:

Mr C buys land worth £10,000 in 1985.
At this time the retail price index was 95.49.

Mr C sells the land in 1997 for £17,000
The retail price index is 158.5.

The inflation factor increase over that period was (158.5 - 95.49) = 63.01.
Divide this by the initial inflation factor of 95.49.

63.01 ÷ 95.49 = 0.659*

Multiply the inflation or *indexation factor* by the original cost of the asset:

0.659 × £10,000 = £6590

So £7000 (the gain) – £6590 (indexation allowance) = £910

Therefore Mr C does not have to pay Capital Gains Tax unless he has other gains that bring the total gains to more than £6500 for the April 1997 to April 1998 tax year.
* Indexation factor is to three decimal places.

Tax warning: You cannot claim to have made a capital loss if that loss was created by deducting the *indexation allowance*. The inflation factor can only reduce profits, not create losses.

Tax tip: The indexation allowance can also be applied to costs in buying the assets and costs of enhancing the asset.

A BASIC COURSE IN CAPITAL GAINS TAX

Note: Indexation will only be given on periods up to April 1998. You can deduct indexation until that date, but no further indexation will be given after that date. Assets acquired on or after 1 April 1998 will get no indexation allowance.

> **Tax tip:** To make the most of the indexation allowance, business assets (purchased on or after 1 April 1998) will have to be held for more than four years, assuming real asset growth rates of 6 per cent and inflation of 2 per cent. Assets sold within four years will suffer a greater Capital Gains Tax liability.

WHAT ELSE CAN I DEDUCT TO REDUCE MY CAPITAL GAIN/PROFIT?

In addition to the effects of inflation and the costs of buying, selling and improving your asset you can deduct losses.

You can offset *losses* suffered on the sale of capital assets from the profits you make on the sales of other assets in the same tax period.

If you make a capital loss you should fill in the Capital Gains Tax section of your Tax Return so that you can offset these losses against any gains in this tax year or in the next tax year or any future year without time limit provided you tell the Inland Revenue that the loss is available to carry forward. So you must make a note on your Tax Return.

If you make a loss on the sale of an asset you must use this to reduce your Capital Gains Tax bill for 1997 to 1998, even if this reduces your gains to less than the £6500 tax-free threshold. Any additional losses should be offset against other income or capital gains in future years. This is known as *carrying forward* losses. You can also bring forward losses from previous years to reduce your capital gains this year. If you carry forward losses they cannot reduce your gains to less than the £6500 tax free threshold.

You must claim losses you make in the 1997 to 1998 tax year, within five years and ten months of the end of the tax year. That means you must use your losses to reduce profits within this time period by 31 January 2004. If you have not included losses in your Tax Return you can do so next year or by telling your Tax Office.

> **Tax tips:**
>
> ☐ If you have made a loss on shares in a trading company (that is **not** quoted on the stock exchange) you can offset this loss against your income to **reduce your income tax** rather than against your capital gain but **only** if you subscribed for new shares.
> ☐ Before selling assets, calculate if they will exceed the £6500 threshold. If they will, try to defer the sale of some assets to the next tax year. If losses reduce your gains to less than the threshold you will lose your tax-free allowance – so defer losses where possible.
> ☐ You can claim as a loss anything that was destroyed or no longer has any value (or negligible value) including shares in companies that have gone into liquidation.
> ☐ You can also claim losses from a business against your Capital Gains Tax.
> ☐ You can use losses from some rented properties (only those classed as furnished holiday lettings) to reduce your Capital Gains Tax liability.

CHATTELS AND WASTING ASSETS

If you buy anything that has a predictable life of 50 years or less on the date on which you acquired it, when you sell it you will **not** pay Capital Gains Tax (provided you have not used it in your business and have or could have claimed capital allowances). These 'wasting assets' can include anything from a racehorse to electronic equipment.

Many 'chattels' also escape Capital Gains Tax. This is a legal term that means an 'item of tangible, moveable property'. This will include items of household furniture, paintings, antiques, items of crockery and china, plate and silverware and any equipment or machinery that is not permanently fixed to the building (anything from your washing machine to your computer).

You only have to pay Capital Gains Tax on these chattels if you sell them for more than **£6000 per item** and only the proceeds over £6000. **Either** calculate the taxable sum by multiplying the sale proceeds above £6000 by 5/3 (in this calculation you cannot make any deductions for costs or indexation).

Or you can calculate the *net gain* by taking the total sale proceeds, not just the amount over £6000, and deducting costs as for other assets. After you have done these two calculations use the **lower** figure when filling out your Tax Return.

A BASIC COURSE IN CAPITAL GAINS TAX

To work out which figure to use see the following example:

How to calculate net gain:	How to calculate gain under £6000 rule
£8000 (sale proceeds) - £2000 (initial purchase price) - £600 (auction fees) - £1000 (indexation) = £4400	£8000 (sale proceeds) - £6000 (allowance) = £2000 x 5/3 = £3333

Tax warnings:

☐ If you made a loss you can only claim losses assuming you received £6000. So if you bought an asset for £8000 and sold it for £5000 you must assume the sale price was £6000. So you can only claim £2000 of losses instead of £3000. If the sale proceeds were above £6000 you can claim the whole loss.

☐ You cannot get round this rule by selling a set of items separately to the same person or group of people. So if you have a set of antique chairs you cannot claim each chair as a separate item. This also applies to matching ornaments, books by the same author or on the same subject, chessmen and sets of silver cutlery. If you want further information ask for Inland Revenue *Help Sheet IR293* from your Tax Office.

CAPITAL GAINS AND YOUR HOME

Your main home is exempt from Capital Gains Tax when you sell it. This is known as *private residence relief*. But there are some exceptions to this rule: ie if you earned money from your home (for instance by renting it out) or used your home for running a business.

If you bought a home and converted it into self-contained flats and sold them off you could be liable to Capital Gains Tax. The same applies if you built a second home in your garden.

If the property has been partially **rented out**, then you could be liable for tax on the area let for the period of the letting. If it was only let for a few years, you will only pay tax on the profits made in some years and on the proportion of the home let.

HOW SMALL AND MEDIUM-SIZED BUSINESSES ARE TAXED

Tax tips:

- **If you rent out or let your property for residential use up to £40,000 of gains may be exempt.** Ask your Tax Office for advice.
- If you have a **lodger** (under the rent-a-room scheme) the whole home will qualify for private residence relief. Only if you have more than one lodger could your home become liable to Capital Gains Tax.
- The final 36 months of ownership of your main home always qualifies as tax exempt (for private residence relief) even if you let the property out during that time.
- Your home may still be regarded as your principle private residence even if you have not been living in it because you have been employed outside the UK or have been forced to live elsewhere because of your job (but not for more than four years).
- If you buy a home but cannot move into it because you are unable to sell your existing home you can own both homes for up to 12 months without being liable for Capital Gains Tax.
- If you work from home – either on a self-employed basis or as an employee – you may be liable to Capital Gains Tax if you use part of your home exclusively for business. To get round this use a room **almost exclusively** for business. You will still be able to claim for heating, light and your telephone and other expenses.

If you are still unsure about your tax situation, ask for *Help Sheet IR282 Private residence relief.*

CAPITAL GAINS AND MARRIED COUPLES

If you give something to your husband or wife no Capital Gains Tax liability arises on this gift providing you are living together. Remember if you give an asset away it is normally treated as though you sold it.

However, if the husband or wife then sells this gift he or she will have to pay Capital Gains Tax from the date the asset was first purchased – not the date the asset was given to the spouse. Ask for *Help Sheet IR281.*

A BASIC COURSE IN CAPITAL GAINS TAX

Tax tips:
- ☐ You can avoid or reduce a Capital Gains Tax bill by making the most of the allowance given to both the husband and wife. If you make a profit of £13,000 (£13,600 for 1988/89) on jointly held assets, by splitting this (putting half on the husband's Tax Return and half on the wife's) you may not have to pay Capital Gains Tax.
- ☐ Married couples can also transfer assets to make the most of a lower tax rate paid by one partner. Remember, Capital Gains Tax is charged at your top rate of tax. If you are a 40 per cent taxpayer you will pay 40 per cent Capital Gains Tax. If you transfer the asset to your spouse, he or she may only pay 20 per cent or 23 per cent Capital Gains Tax. As rates reduce for assets held for more than a year from April 1998, lower-rate taxpayers will still pay less than high-rate taxpayers.
- ☐ Transfer assets to your spouse so that you can both use up your £6500 allowance (£6800 for 1988/99).

Tax warning: If you are about to divorce part of your settlement may mean you have to transfer assets to your spouse. Transfers between spouses are only exempt if you are still married and living together. Make sure you take account of any potential tax liability when reaching your divorce settlement.

OTHER RELIEFS THAT REDUCE YOUR CAPITAL GAINS TAX BILL

If you make a gift, dispose of a home you have provided for a dependent relative, have sold an asset outside the UK but are unable to transfer the proceeds to the UK or have paid Capital Gains Tax in a foreign country ask your Tax Office for the relevant *Help Sheets*.

HOW TO REDUCE YOUR CAPITAL GAINS ON THE SALE OF A BUSINESS OR BUSINESS ASSET

There are several tax reliefs available to those running their own business.

Generally you have to pay Capital Gains Tax on the sale of a business or a business asset if you are self-employed. The same applies to partnerships.

However, most business assets, such as computers or office furniture, do not result in gains as they depreciate in value. These are covered by capital allowances/balancing charges, which are covered in depth in Part 2, Chapter 9. So the sale of an item of office furniture or other plant and machinery will be covered by this section of your Tax Return, not under the Capital Gains Tax section.

Retirement relief

This valuable relief is being phased out following the March 1998 Budget. It will gradually reduce from 6 April 1999 and will cease to be available from 6 April 2003. It will take some time for the tapering reductions in Capital Gains Tax to filter through, so many businesses may find that they face a larger Capital Gains liability.

Despite its name you do not have to retire to benefit from this. The relief is given on the sale of your business or a material part of your business or any assets which were used in your business at the time it ceased. It applies to those selling a business they have run for at least a year or business assets that have been used in your business for at least a year. You can obtain the relief once you are **age 50** (if disposal is pre-28 November 1995 the qualifying age is 55) or if you are retiring on the grounds of ill-health. You must sell a distinct part of your business' not just a small part of it.

The relief is given to the self-employed running their own business, those in partnership and those who own at least 5 per cent of the voting rights of a company they work for as a director or employee. These are known as *personal trading companies*. If you sell shares in a personal trading company only a proportion of the shares sold may be eligible for retirement relief so ask your Tax Office for advice.

You will receive:

☐ 100 per cent relief on the first £250,000 of gains in 1998/99 redundancy to £200,000 in 1999/2000 and to £50,000 in 2002/03;
☐ 50 per cent on further gains up to £1,000,000 in 1998/99, reducing to £200,000 in 2002/03;
☐ giving a maximum relief of £625,000 in 1998/99.

But you can only claim the maximum if you have owned the asset for long enough. If you have owned the business for one year the percentage of the £250,000 that is exempt is 10 per cent so you can deduct £25,000 from your gains. Each year the amount of relief you can claim rises by a further 15 per cent, so after five years this percentage rises to 50 per cent and after ten years to 100 per cent.

> **Tax tips:**
>
> ☐ If you have run two or more businesses in succession and have only run the last business for less than a year you can still claim retirement relief by adding the past periods of business together. Ask your Tax Office for *Help Sheet IR289* for more details on retirement relief.
>
> ☐ If you make the most of retirement relief it can mean that you pay **no** Capital Gains Tax on the sale of a business. Husbands and wives are each eligible for the relief so they can each have a maximum of £625,000 of relief for 1998/99. If you acquired the whole of your spouse's business interest you may be able to elect to have retirement relief calculated over the joint period in business. If you and your wife jointly own 5 per cent of a personal trading company, but neither owns the minimum 5 per cent to qualify for retirement relief, consider transferring the shares to one partner so the whole gain is exempt.

Roll-over relief

Roll-over relief allows you to defer gains made on the sale of business assets **if** replacement assets are bought. If you sell your shop and buy a new one, you can ask not to pay tax on the sale of the old shop until you have sold the new one. The same applies to land that is compulsory purchased. You can roll-over the gain if you buy new land. You have to make this claim by filling in a form attached to Inland Revenue *Help Sheet IR290*.

> **Tax tip:** Wherever possible, and until it is phased out, opt for retirement relief rather than roll-over relief because the former exempts you from tax whereas the latter only defers your tax.

Roll-over relief can be claimed by the self-employed who are 'trading', including those renting out furnished holiday lettings and those who own at least 5 per cent of the voting rights of their own company.

If you are trading you can **only** claim the relief if you use the old and new assets in the same trade or another trade that you already carry on or start within three years. Only:

HOW SMALL AND MEDIUM-SIZED BUSINESSES ARE TAXED

- ☐ buildings,
- ☐ land,
- ☐ fixed plant and machinery,
- ☐ goodwill, and
- ☐ certain milk quotas and potato quotas

can be claimed.

Relief is given by carrying forward the gain and deducting it from the cost of the new asset. To get full relief, the whole amount of the proceeds from the sale of the original asset must be reinvested. If you only reinvest part of the gain you will be liable to Capital Gains Tax immediately on the lower of the full gain and the amount equal to the proceeds not reinvested. The new asset qualifies for indexation allowance from the date of purchase (up to April 1998, when this allowance was scrapped).

Where the new asset is a *depreciating asset* (it is or will become a wasting asset within the next ten years or is fixed plant or machinery), the gain is not rolled over permanently. It is deferred until the earliest of disposal of the new asset, ten years after the new asset was bought or the date the new asset ceases to be used in the trade. This rule, therefore, covers all assets with an expected life of no more than 60 years.

Business transfer relief

Business transfer relief defers the gain made when you transfer a business in exchange for shares, for instance if you decide to incorporate your business (become a company). You do not need to claim this relief. To qualify the business including all its assets (other than cash) must be transferred as a going concern and in return you must receive shares.

Relief is reduced if you receive cash and shares. This relief can be avoided by retaining a non-cash asset. You may want to do this if your gain is small and as such you want to pay a small amount of Capital Gains Tax on the transfer, but you will not get a reduction in the costs you can claim when you sell the shares at a later date (you will suffer a larger Capital Gains Tax bill as a result).

Note: There is no equivalent relief if the business transfers from a company to a sole trader. If only part of the business is transfered to a company (eg you retain a freehold property) then no relief is given.

A BASIC COURSE IN CAPITAL GAINS TAX

Reinvestment relief

This applies when you use the capital gain to invest in an unquoted trading company or another business if you are self-employed or in partnership. You reduce your gain by the amount of the gain you reinvest. So if your total capital gains are £50,000 and you invested £35,000 your taxable gain is reduced to £15,000. Shares must be in an unquoted trading company (not quoted on the stock exchange but including those quoted on the Alternative Investment Market – AIM) and there are some restrictions on the type of trade in which you can invest. Commodities, futures, shares and securities firms are ineligible as are businesses dealing in land and those providing financial, legal or accountancy services.

> **Tax tip:** If you reinvest your gains in an Enterprise Investment Scheme, you can put in up to £150,000, defer your Capital Gains and get 20 per cent tax relief on the amount invested.

Holdover relief

Holdover relief enables you to avoid paying tax on a gift by transferring your Capital Gains Tax liability to the person who receives the gift. Assets which qualify include:

- business assets used in a profession, trade or vocation of the person making the gift;
- shares in unquoted trading companies, family businesses or other business in which the donor has at least 5 per cent of the voting rights in the shares;
- agricultural property.

The relief works by allowing you to give an asset at no gain or loss (the price you paid plus any extra costs in purchasing it). The recipient then calculates their capital gains, using the market value at the time of transfer, less the gains held over. This can be useful if a business is handed down to the next generation. However, Inheritance Tax could still be payable if the donor dies within seven years of making the gift. If the donor also gets retirement relief, the held over gain is the amount remaining after retirement relief.

Losses on loans made to traders

Losses on loans made to traders also qualify for tax relief as these losses can be used to reduce your Capital Gains Tax liability. Loans or guarantees of loans, must be lent wholly for the purposes of trade and the debt must not be a debt on a security such as a debenture loan. The rules also allow you to get relief for money used to set up a business which you subsequently run. But you cannot lend money to your spouse. The money must be irrecoverable to qualify and only the lost principal of the loan can be claimed, not lost interest. Ask for *Help Sheet IR296*.

> **Tax tip:** You can also claim losses from a business to reduce your Capital Gains Tax liability arising from the sale of non-business assets as well as business assets.

If you are in **partnership** you are responsible for reporting any capital gains arising on the sale of your interests in assets of the partnership. So if your business sold its business premises, you must declare your share. Remember when you leave a partnership you are classed as disposing of your share of the assets of that partnership. If a new partner joins or one leaves your share of the assets may also change so you may have made a gain. Ask your Tax Office for *Help Sheet IR228*.

LEASES

If you sell your lease, or grant a lease out of a freehold, you may also be liable for Capital Gains Tax. Long leases (those with more than 50 years to run) are not wasting assets and therefore treated as normal disposals for capital gains. For short-leases the calculation is more complicated. Instead of an inflation/indexation allowance, short leases are written down – assuming less depreciation in the first years and greater depreciation as the lease nears its end.

If you grant a short lease, part of the premium is deemed to be property income under Schedule A but the amount taxed under Schedule A is deducted when calculating your capital gain.

If you grant a long lease or sub-lease out of head lease of freehold, this is treated as a part-disposal under capital gains.

3

A BASIC GUIDE TO NATIONAL INSURANCE CONTRIBUTIONS

The only National Insurance contributions assessed by your Tax Return are Class 4 contributions for the self-employed. Class 2 contributions must be paid directly to the Contributions Agency which is part of the Department of Social Security.

The March 1998 Budget proposed the abolition of Class 2 Contributions and an increase in the Class 4 rate, which will have to be paid in profits well below the current threshold. As such the self-employed will pay more than they currently contribute in National Insurance.

WARNING: You may be prosecuted if you fail to pay any NI contributions for which you are liable.

CLASS 2 NI CONTRIBUTIONS

Currently these must be paid by the self-employed for each week of self-employment including holiday periods if you:
- are normally self-employed **and**
- are aged 16 and over **and**
- are under pension age **and**
- have not been excepted from liability to pay Class 2 NI contributions.

Those with small earnings

If your earnings are below £3590 for the tax year 1998/99 you can apply to be excepted from liability to pay Class 2 contributions. You should apply before the start of the tax year. If you do not, your certificate of exemption can only usually be backdated for up to 13

HOW SMALL AND MEDIUM-SIZED BUSINESSES ARE TAXED

weeks and cannot be issued to cover any week for which you have already paid Class 2 NICs. If you cannot do this (partly because you are unsure whether your earnings will be below the threshold) you can apply for a refund but you must apply by 31 December following the end of the tax year in question.

Ask for leaflet CA02: *National Insurance contributions for self-employed people with small earnings* from your local Contributions Agency (see your telephone directory).

Credits

These protect your NI record for the state retirement pension and widow's benefit as well as maintaining your entitlement to other benefits.

You may be able to get credits instead of paying Class 2 NI contributions if you are:

- sick for a full calendar week (from Sunday to Saturday) not part of a week and you will normally have to send in sick notes to your local Social Security office;
- entitled to maternity allowance, invalid care allowance or unemployability supplement;
- entitled to statutory sick pay or statutory maternity pay;
- taking a course of approved training;
- receiving disability working allowance;
- required to attend jury services.

> **Tax tips:**
>
> - As the rate of Class 2 National Insurance is low (see Table 3.1) you may want to make voluntary payments so that you still qualify for the state benefits they provide.
> - If you are sick and unable to work for a complete (but not part of a) week, Sunday to Saturday, you do not have to pay contributions and may be able to get credits for complete weeks of sickness.

Table 3.1 *Class 2 National Insurance contribution rates (1998/99 tax year)*

Class 2 Contributions	1997/1998
Per week flat rate	£6.35
Small earnings exception – if your annual earnings are below this limit you can apply for an exemption	£3590.00

WARNING: You are liable to pay contributions even if they are too late to count for benefit purposes. NI contributions not paid until the second tax year after the one in which they were due may be charged at a higher rate. Ask for leaflet *CA07: National Insurance – unpaid and late paid contributions*.

Until Class 2 NICs are combined with Class 4 contributions from 1999 they will count towards the following benefits:

- incapacity benefit (paid to the self-employed if unable to work for four days or more);
- retirement pension;
- widow's benefit;
- maternity allowance.

They do **not** count towards contribution-based Jobseeker's Allowance.

CLASS 3 NATIONAL INSURANCE CONTRIBUTIONS

The self-employed can opt to pay these on a voluntary basis (see Table 3.2) to help them qualify for some benefits. This will be in cases where:

- you are not liable to pay NI contributions;
- you have been excepted from paying Class 2 NI contributions;
- your contribution record is not good enough.

Table 3.2 *Class 3 National Insurance contributions*

Voluntary Contributions (Class 3 Contributions)	1998/1999
Per Week	£6.05

Tax tip: If you fit into one of the above categories it may be worth paying Class 3 NICs. If your National Insurance contributions are not high enough in each qualifying year, they will not count towards the retirement pension or widow's benefits. As a result you could retire with a reduced pension.

CLASS 4 NATIONAL INSURANCE CONTRIBUTIONS

These are paid by the self-employed on **profits** over a certain amount. They are paid in addition to Class 2 contributions. Only the following do **not** have to pay Class 4 contributions or can apply for an exemption:
- those over pensionable age at the **beginning** of the year of assessment;
- those not resident in the UK for income tax purposes during the year of assessment;
- 'sleeping partners' – those who supply capital and take a share of profits but take no active part in running the business;
- trustees, executors and administrators (in some cases only).

You pay Class 4 contributions as a percentage of your **taxable profits**. Note that this will probably be different from the profits in your accounts as items such as losses, capital allowances and balancing charges are used to calculate your taxable profits but may not be included when working out the profits listed in your accounts. (These terms are explained in Part 2.)

The income you pay Class 4 NICs on is:

- your business profits as calculated for income tax, including any adjustments for capital allowances and balancing charges; plus
- any enterprise allowance you receive in the first 52 weeks of trade.

You can deduct from your income:

- Certain annual payments, known as trade charges (for instance a patent royalty), if they are *wholly and exclusively* for the purpose of the business and have not been deducted in working out the business profits for tax purposes. If the amount you deduct exceeds the profits you made in the year, the balance can be carried forward and deducted from future profits.
- Trading losses can be given in a number of ways, either:
  – set against income of the same or previous year;
  – set against future income of the same trade;
  – and if the loss was in any of the first four years of the business it can be set against the three previous years' income;

– you can deduct trading losses even if they have previously been offset against non-trading income.

Class 4 contributions are calculating using information on your Tax Return (you will have to calculate these yourself or get your accountant to do so if you do not send back your Tax Return by 30 September 1988). Unlike other NICs they are paid to the Inland Revenue instead of the Contributions Agency and are paid at the same time as your tax bill. See Table 3.3 for the 1997/98 rate of contribution.

Note: You can no longer tax deduct half your Class 4 NICs as a business expense. 1995/96 was the last year that this was allowed.

If you are in partnership your Class 4 NICs are based on your profits from the partnership.

When calculating your trading profits do not take into account:

☐ personal tax allowances;
☐ retirement annuity relief, personal pensions relief and superannuation contributions.

Table 3.3 *Class 4 National Insurance Contributions*

Class 4 contributions	1997/1998	1998/99
Lower profits limit (per year) – no NI contributions payable on profits & gains below this limit	£7010	£7310
Upper profits limit (per year) – no NI contributions payable on profits and gains above this limit	£24,180	£25,220
Rate of all contributions payable	6%	6%
Maximum contributions payable	£1030.20	£1074.60

Note: Contributions are only paid on profits above the lower profits threshold.

> **Tax tip:** If you have earnings from employment and self-employment there is a maximum amount of NI contributions you can make in a year. If you pay the maximum NI contributions from employment (£2201.62 for the 1997/98 tax year) you will not have to pay any Class 4 contributions. You can apply for a deferment of contributions before the start of the tax year for which the Class 4 contributions will be due. If, once your Class 4

HOW SMALL AND MEDIUM-SIZED BUSINESSES ARE TAXED

> contributions have been added to your Class 1 contributions from employment, you exceed this limit you can apply for a refund of Class 4 contributions at the end of the tax year. The maximum amount of Class 1, Class 2 and Class 4 NI contributions you can pay in the 1997/98 tax year is £1356.15.

How Class 4 NICs are calculated for the 1997/98 tax year:

Trading profits	£20,000	
Less: Capital allowances	(£5000)	
Less: Loss carried forward	(£1000)	
		£14,000
Less: Lower profits limit		(£7010)
Class 4 NICs payable on		£6990
This is below the upper profit limit of £24,180		
So contributions are: 6% @ £6990		£419.40

Making payments

Payments are due in the same way as income tax with two payments in instalments and then a final balancing payment. The deadlines for payments for the 1997/98 tax year are:

- 31 January 1998 first payment *on account*;
- 31 July 1998 second payment *on account*;
- 31 January 1999 balancing payment.

Note that not everyone needs to make payments on account. Payments are based on the net Income Tax and Class 4 NI contributions due for the previous year after taking into account any tax deducted at source. You do not need to make a payment on account if:

- each payment would be less than £250; or
- 80 per cent of the Income Tax and Class 4 NICs for the previous year was met by tax deducted at source (for instance, under the SC60 scheme for contractors).

WARNING: If payment is overdue you will have to pay interest.

CLASS 1 NATIONAL INSURANCE CONTRIBUTIONS

Although these are not paid by the self-employed (unless they also have earnings from employment), if you are or become an employer you will have to deduct NICs from your employees' wages **and** pay an employer's contribution (see Table 3.4).

Employer's and employees' National Insurance contributions are **not** paid or deducted using the information supplied on your Tax Return. You must pay contributions within set time limits directly to the Inland Revenue (see Chapter 6 on employing staff). However, you **can** deduct tax and NICs paid as employer as a tax-deductible expense when calculating your business profits and when filling out your Tax Return.

Table 3.4 *Class 1 National Insurance Contributions*

Employees and employers (Class 1 Contributions)	1998/1999
Lower earnings limit per week – employees and employers do not pay NI contributions if weekly earnings are below this limit (up to £63.99)	£64.00
Upper earnings limit per week – employees do not pay NI contributions on earnings above this limit	£485.00
Employee rates If your earnings exceed the lower earnings limit, you pay the *initial* rate on earnings up to the limit (£64) and *standard* rate on earnings over this limit (up to the upper earnings limit of £485)	2% initial 10% standard (8.4% standard if a member of a company pension scheme contracted out of SERPS)

Employer rates If earnings are within the range:	First £64:	On remainder:
Up to £64	None	None
£64 to £109.99	3% on all earnings	
£110 to £154.99	5% on all earnings	
£155 to £209.99	7% on all earnings	
£210 to £485	10% on all earnings	
Over £485	10% on all earnings	

Employer rates if employee is in contract-out pension scheme If earnings are within the range:	First £62:	On remainder:
Up to £64	None	None
£64 to £109.99	3%	None
£110 to £154.99	5%	2 %
£155 to £209.99	7%	4 %
£210 to £485	10%	7 %
Over £485	10%	7 % on £210 – £485 then 10%

HOW SMALL AND MEDIUM-SIZED BUSINESSES ARE TAXED

Note: From April 1999 the starting rate for NICs will rise to over £81 a week and above this employers' contributions will be at a rate of 12.2 per cent.

> **Tax tip:** If you are considering employing staff, pay them just below the £64 a week threshold and you will not have to deduct NI contributions. Alternatively pay them just below one of the other NIC thresholds to save on NI contributions.

USEFUL CONTACTS

For more information about Class 2 NICs or paying quarterly bills, ring the Self Employment Directorate Call Centre on 06451 56921. Calls are charged at BT local rate. You can also contact the Contributions Agency, Self Employment Directorate (either the Quarterly Billing Section or the Direct Debit Section), Longbenton, Newcastle upon Tyne, NE98 1YX.

For more information about Schedule D tax (self-employment tax) and related Class 4 NICs contact your local Tax Enquiry Centre or Tax Office.

4

A BASIC GUIDE TO VAT

VAT is **not** dealt with by the Inland Revenue and as such is not calculated and collected using the information you supply on your Tax Return. However, if you are **not** registered for VAT, you can include the VAT element of the cost of allowable expenses and assets when deducting these from turnover to arrive at profits.

REGISTERING FOR VAT

VAT is payable to Customs & Excise by all *taxable persons* – those registered for VAT carrying on a business with *taxable supplies*. These are goods and services that are not exempt (see the list later in this chapter). VAT is charged at two rates: 17.5 per cent and a zero-rate of 0 per cent. Note that there is a difference between zero-rated and exempt. For a start you cannot generally recover VAT on goods or services bought to make or supply anything that is exempt.

Unlike Income Tax, VAT is charged on your *taxable turnover* not your profits. Not all businesses need to register for VAT. It is **compulsory** to *register* if, at the end of any calendar month, the value of *taxable supplies* (excluding VAT) over **the last 12 months** up to that date has exceeded £49,000 – the new threshold from 1 December 1997 – or if taxable supplies are likely to exceed £49,000 in the next month. (A list of what constitutes taxable supplies is given later in this chapter.) So you will probably find that your VAT accounts run over a different period to your business accounts. You must notify your liability to register on form *VAT 1*.

Note: This means that the period over which the VAT threshold test applies is **any** 12 months, **not** the tax year, accounting year or a calendar year.

HOW SMALL AND MEDIUM-SIZED BUSINESSES ARE TAXED

Tax tips:

- When you apply for registration you can ask Customs to allocate tax periods which fit in with your own financial year or to have tax periods allocated to cover accounting systems not based on calendar months.
- If you are a non-registered trader you should review your taxable turnover at the end of every calendar month to ensure you have not exceeded the registration threshold. If you exceed the threshold you must notify Customs of your liability to register within 30 days of the end of that month. Registration then takes effect from the following month.
- VAT incurred before registration can be treated as input tax and recovered from Customs provided the goods or services were acquired/supplied for the same business that is registered and have not been supplied onwards (in the case of goods) or were supplied within six months prior to the date of registration (in the cases of services).
- You may be able to avoid compulsory registration if you can demonstrate to Customs that your taxable turnover will be less than £47,000 in the following 12 months.

Note: that the threshold for *deregistration* from VAT is £47,000 – not £49,000, the threshold for registration. In certain cases deregistration is compulsory including:

- if you cease to make taxable goods or services (notification must be within 30 days);
- if your business status changes – for instance a sole trader becomes a partnership or is incorporated into a company.

On deregistration, VAT is chargeable on all stocks and capital assets.

Tax warning:

- You are also liable to register for VAT if there are reasonable grounds for believing that taxable supplies (excluding VAT) will exceed £49,000 in the following 30 days.
- If an ongoing business is transferred to you and you are not registered for VAT, you must take into account the supplies of the transferred business when determining whether the VAT limit is exceeded.
- You cannot get round the VAT threshold rules by splitting your business or operating what is effectively one business through separate entities. There are anti-avoidance provisions to prevent this and **all** taxable income must be aggregated when determining liability to register for VAT – no matter how diverse the businesses.

A BASIC GUIDE TO VAT

> **Tax tips:**
>
> - [ ] If you earn less than this registration threshold you can ask to voluntarily register for VAT. You will gain if the goods or services you supply are **not** exempt from VAT and are zero rated and you have *input VAT* (VAT on goods and services which you have paid for) which you want to reclaim and this input VAT is greater than your *output VAT*, the amount you must charge on sale of the goods or services and pay over to Customs and Excise. But a word of warning: your customers may not want VAT to be charged – particularly if they are not VAT registered – and you must **not** underestimate the administrative burden of VAT registration.
> - [ ] Likewise if you are VAT-registered it may be worth your while encouraging suppliers to be VAT-registered as you can then reclaim input tax.
> - [ ] If the goods or services you supply are zero-rated but in excess of the compulsory registration threshold, you can request an exemption. But this is only advisable where the net amount of VAT you can recover is small and as such is worth forgoing to save on the administration involved in complying with VAT requirements.

Note: if you are in *partnership* the aggregate profits of the business are taken as the turnover, not the individual profits of each partner.

Once you know that you are required to register you must start keeping VAT records and charging VAT to customers. But VAT should not be shown separately on any invoices until the registration number is known. A VAT invoice should be forwarded once the registration number is known detailing how much VAT has been charged.

HOW VAT IS CHARGED

VAT is charged at each stage of the manufacturing or service process with registered traders deducting any VAT they suffer (input tax) from the tax which they charge to their customers (output tax) before making VAT payments to Customs & Excise.

For example:

> Business A sells £1000 of raw materials to Business B and charges £175 VAT.
>
> Business B sells these goods to a retailer for £1500 plus VAT of £262.50.
>
> Business B then pays VAT of:
>
> £262.50 (output tax) - £175 (input tax) = £87.50

When accounting for VAT you must use the *tax point* as the date of supply. Known as the *basic tax point*, this is usually the date on which goods are made available or services completed. However, this is not always the case.

- If the tax invoice is issued or payment is received before the basic tax point, this date becomes the tax point.
- If the tax invoice is issued within 14 days after the basic tax point, use the invoice date (unless you have specified that the basic tax point be used). This 14-day period may be extended to accommodate monthly invoicing with Custom's permission. The invoice date or end of the month then becomes the tax point.
- Goods supplied on sale or return are supplied on the earlier of acceptance/adoption by the customer or 12 months after despatch.
- Continuous supplies of services paid for periodically are charged on the earlier of receipt of payment or issue of tax invoice. Note this is different from the annual accounting for small businesses with turnovers up to £350,000.

ZERO-RATED, EXEMPT AND STANDARD RATE VAT

Generally, if goods or services are not exempt or zero-rated, then the standard rate of VAT of 17.5 per cent must be charged (apart from the special 5 per cent rate for domestic fuel and power). Note that if your goods and services are exempt you cannot reclaim any input tax (VAT paid by you on goods and services you have bought).

The following are *zero-rated* (note, as this is only a basic guide to VAT, so this is not a comprehensive list):

- food, but not luxury items such as confectionery or those supplied in the course of catering;
- books, periodicals and leaflets but not stationery;
- new construction work/the sale of new residential buildings;
- passenger transport but not pleasure transport or transport in vehicles seating fewer than 12 passengers;
- drugs and medicines on prescription;
- exports of goods to outside the EU;
- supplies to VAT registered traders in other EU states;
- clothing and footwear for young children.

Exempt supplies include:

- freehold sales of land and buildings unless:
  – zero rated; or
  – commercial buildings less than three years old (these are standard rated);
- leasehold sales of land and buildings;
- financial services but not investment advice which is standard rated;
- insurance (although insurance is subject to insurance premium tax);
- postal services provided by the Post Office;
- education and health services.

Mixed and *composite* supplies are those that are a mixed supply of goods or services, some of which are standard-rated and some of which are zero-rated or exempt. You must account for tax separately on the various elements unless it is a *composite supply,* for instance an airline flight which is zero-rated as transport and a meal which is standard rated. In this case, the rate of the supply as a whole is taken – as the meal is only incidental. But, to take an extreme example, if you sold a meal with a flight to the restaurant included and the meal was the main expense, VAT would have to be charged as catering is taxable at the standard rate.

When you are accounting for *input tax* on mixed supplies there is a set calculation used by Customs:

1. Calculate the total amount of input tax.
2. Calculate the amount of input tax you have paid on goods and services to make taxable supplies.
3. Calculate the amount of input tax which relates to exempt supplies (this is not recoverable).

HOW SMALL AND MEDIUM-SIZED BUSINESSES ARE TAXED

4. Calculate the remaining input tax which cannot be attributed directly to either 2 or 3.

For example:

Input tax attributed	
to taxable supplies	£10,000
to exempt supplies	£5000
Unattributed	£35,000
Total	£55,000

One-quarter of the supplies made by this business are exempt and three-quarters are taxable. Use turnover excluding VAT when doing this calculation.

Taxable turnover divided by total turnover × 100% = the percentage of unattributed input VAT you can reclaim. (Round the percentage to the nearest whole figure.)

So if taxable turnover is 75 per cent this business can reclaim:

75% × £35,000 (of input tax) = £26,250 plus the £10,000 paid on taxable supplies = £36,250 out of a total input tax of £55,000.

Alternative calculations such as the ratio of the number of taxable transaction to the total number of transactions can be used by agreement with Customs.

Some incidental items of expenditure that are exempt are regarded as taxable when doing the partial exemption calculation above including deposit interest. Ask your local Customs office for advice on which calculation to use and what should be included.

Second-hand goods come under a separate set of rules. VAT is only charged on the seller's margin – the difference between the selling price and the cost to them.

> **Tax tip:** If part of your goods or services are exempt and others taxable, you can only recover VAT on supplies attributable to the taxable goods or services. However, there is a *de minimis* limit. So if the total input tax attributable to exempt supplies is below £625 per month on average it is treated as being attributable to taxable supplies and is fully recoverable. The annual limit is £7500.

VAT YOU CANNOT CLAIM BACK

VAT on some items cannot be deductible for input tax:

- [ ] motor cars – unless acquired new for resale, leasing or in a taxi, self-drive, car hire or driving school business;
- [ ] business entertaining;
- [ ] non-business items passed through the business account;
- [ ] items bought partly for business use and partly for private use in which case only the business proportion of input tax can be deducted.

Special rules for those buying cars for use in their business

VAT is only recoverable on cars bought *wholly* for business purposes (ie for resale unused) and VAT must also be charged on the sale of the cars. So in most cases you cannot reclaim VAT on the purchase of company cars, but you can reclaim any VAT charged on repair and maintenance costs without apportionment for private use.

If an employee makes a payment for use of the car, output tax must be accounted for on this payment.

VAT incurred on fuel used for business purposes is fully reclaimable even if incurred by the employee. However, if fuel is supplied for private use at less than the cost of the fuel to the business, all input tax is recoverable but you must account for output tax using set scale private mileage charges unless you apply for a concession and do not reclaim any input tax on the fuel. These scale charges are the same as the Income Tax Mileage scale charges on private fuel for company car drivers.

VAT YOU CAN CLAIM BACK

Tax tips:

- [ ] Do not forget to reclaim a refund of VAT on bad debts if you have already accounted for it and paid tax on the goods or services, have written off the debts in your accounts and six months have elapsed from the date of supply.

> ☐ Do not forget to write off input tax which is irrecoverable in your profit and loss account. It can be included in the cost of expenses or when calculating capital allowances or Capital Gains Tax.

VAT INVOICES

When issuing invoices to another VAT-registered trader you must include specific items of information including:

- ☐ your VAT number
- ☐ date of issue, tax point and invoice number;
- ☐ type of supply;
- ☐ description of goods or services;
- ☐ the rate of tax and tax exclusive amount;
- ☐ total invoice price excluding VAT with separate totals for zero-rated and exempt supplies;
- ☐ each VAT rate applicable and the amount of VAT at each rate; and
- ☐ the total amount of VAT.

However, if you are a *retailer* and the invoice is for £100 or less including VAT you do not have to include so much detail, only the rate of tax and amount of tax, and you do not have to include zero-rated or exempt supplies on these invoices.

Wholesalers can compute the value of their taxable supplies under one of several special schemes depending on whether their goods and services are all standard rated or are mixed. Ask your local Customs office for details.

Second-hand goods also have their own scheme which limits the amount of tax due to the trader's margin rather than the entire sales price.

VAT RETURNS

VAT is charged over *tax periods* (normally three calendar months long) with returns showing the total input and output tax. These returns must be submitted within one month of the end of this period.

> **Tax tip:** If your input tax will regularly exceed output tax – for instance if you make largely zero-rated supplies and are therefore termed a *repayment trader* – you can ask for a one-month tax period to speed up

A BASIC GUIDE TO VAT

> repayments. But you must then balance the additional work involved in making 12 returns per year (instead of four) against the advantage of obtaining more rapid repayments of tax.

VAT returns consist of nine boxes and should be sent to Customs within one month of the end of each tax period with any tax due. If the bank credit transfer system is used, an extra seven days is allowed for the return but not the payment. All input and output tax figures must be supported by invoices and records, including the VAT account, which must be maintained for six years. **Note**: photocopies of invoices are not always acceptable.

> **Tax tip:** If you make an error on your VAT return and it is for less than £2000 you can make a voluntary disclosure using form VAT 652 and escape default interest.

SPECIAL RULES FOR SMALL BUSINESSES

Annual accounting scheme

Businesses with a turnover that does not exceed £300,000 (excluding VAT) can submit only one annual VAT return. There are major administrative savings in this scheme but it is only available to those who regularly pay VAT to Customs, not those who reclaim VAT. Throughout the year you will be required to make payments *on account*, advance payments similar to the advance Income Tax payments made to the Inland Revenue. As with Income Tax, these payments on account are based on the past performance of the business. Traders pay 90 per cent of the estimated VAT due during the year in nine monthly direct debits starting in the fourth month of the VAT year. Any outstanding amount is calculated when completing your annual VAT return and you must submit this along with any payment within two months of the end of the year.

If your turnover is below £100,000 you only have to make quarterly interim payments of 20 per cent of the previous year's net VAT liability. If these are below £2000, you can choose not to make interim payments.

Note: It is **not** possible to register for the annual accounting scheme if you are a repayment trader, ie you claim back more VAT than you pay. And even if you could it would not be advisable as you would have a long delay before receiving any repayment of VAT.

If your taxable supplies exceed £375,000 by the end of the year you must leave the scheme.

Cash accounting

This can be used by businesses whose annual taxable turnover (exclusive of VAT) is £350,000 or lower. The advantage is that the business can account for tax on cash paid and received rather than date of delivery or date of invoice. So you do not have to account for VAT until you receive payment and you cannot recover VAT on purchases until you have paid for them. If your turnover exceeds £437,000 in the 12 months to the end of the VAT accounting period, you must leave the scheme.

> **Tax warning:** Customs has tightened the rules governing the cash accounting scheme to stop businesses using the scheme as a free loan. Business can no longer use the scheme for sales of goods and services invoiced in advance of supply being made, or for sales where payment is not due for more than six months after the date of the invoice. These measures stop the purchaser from claiming an early input tax credit long before the seller makes any supply or has to account for the tax to Customs.

OVERSEAS TRADE

If you are trading with other EU member states special rules apply. If both businesses are registered for VAT, the seller zero rates goods and services and the buyer pays VAT at his country's rate on the supply and then treats this as input tax – this is known as the 'destination' system. If you sell goods to an unregistered EU business simply add UK VAT in the normal way – this is known as the 'origin' system. If you are an unregistered trader buying from a EU business that is VAT registered, VAT will be added at the seller's country's rate. However, no VAT is charged if you buy zero-rated goods from another EU country. If your annual trade (sales and purchases) within the EU is £225,000 or more (the new limit from 1 January 1998) you must submit monthly statistical returns (Intrastat forms) and most traders must also submit EU sales statements quarterly, monthly or annually. There are special rules for mail-order firms selling to individuals in other EU states.

If you buy goods from outside the EU you must add VAT to the goods (including packaging, freight, insurance and excise duties) and account for this at the point of entry to the UK. You then reclaim this tax as input tax on your next VAT return. So you add VAT as though you supplied the goods, even though you acquired them. The rules for purchasing services from non-EU companies are slightly more complicated. But certain services are also treated as though supplied by the UK business which has purchased them. This is known as the reverse charge system.

Exports of goods to outside the EU are zero-rated including goods supplied to visitors from outside the EU.

CHECKING A VAT NUMBER

There is a simple check to find out if a VAT number is false or not. Take the first seven numbers of the VAT registration number and multiply the first by 8, the second by 7 and so on until you get to the seventh which is multiplied by 2. Add up this total. Then deduct 97 until you get to a negative number. This one is the check number.

For example:

> VAT registration number: 876 5432 88
>
> Multiply the figures like this:
> $8 \times 8 + 7 \times 7 + 6 \times 6 + 5 \times 5 + 4 \times 4 + 3 \times 3 + 2 \times 2 = 203 - 97 = 106 - 97 = 9 - 97 = -88$

5

ACCOUNTS AND TAX

As discussed earlier in this book, if you are self-employed it will pay you to employ an accountant not only because you can deduct accountancy costs as an allowable expense from your profits but also so that you do not fall foul of the Inland Revenue.

This chapter has been included so that you can understand the importance of the terms involved, accounting and record keeping. For instance, in your accounts you must include all goods and services you have supplied, not just those you have been paid for. Likewise you must not include payments made for goods and services sold in the previous accounting year. Stocktaking is also important as you can deduct the *cost of sales* (for instance raw materials or goods for resale). And so are accurate details of expenses as some are disallowable (cannot be deducted to reduce your tax bill).

Your accounts must be made up in line with accounting standards. However, when filling in your Tax Return you may have to *adjust* the profits listed in your accounts as some items are not tax deductible and others must be calculated separately. This is because your *net profit* shown in your accounts is usually different from your *taxable trading profit*.

You should already know your *accounting year*, usually a 12-month period ending on your *accounting date*, the date up to which your accounts are drawn up.

When filling in your 1997/98 Tax Return you must include profits, expenses and other deductions for your accounting year **ending** in the tax year. So that will be profits to your accounting date falling between 6 April 1997 and 5 April 1998.

Note: This is known as the *current year basis*. All business are now taxed on this basis but previously, those set up on or before 5 April 1994 were taxed on a preceding year basis and included their accounting year which ended in the previous tax year on their Tax Return. The 1996/97 tax year was a transitional year in which

ACCOUNTS AND TAX

businesses moved to the current year basis.
This is what your accounts should look like:

		[£]	[£]
Sales			X
Less:	Cost of sales:		
	Opening stock	X	
	Purchases	X	
		X	
	Less: Closing stock	(X)	
			(X)
Gross profit			X
Less:	Wages (staff, not yours)	X	
	Rent and rates	X	
	Light and heat	X	
	Professional charges	X	
	Sundry expenses	X	
	Travel	X	
	Entertaining	X	
	Bad debts	X	
	Depreciation	X	
	Management salary	X	
	Bank charges and Interest	X	
	HP Interest	X	
			(X)
Net profit for the year			X

The items listed in your accounts may vary slightly from this. Items of capital expenditure should be calculated separately as they are deducted separately when filling in your Tax Return.

Even though your accounts are drawn up in this correct way, you will find that when it comes to filling in your Tax Return you will have to exclude some of the items you have listed.

When you adjust your profits you must always start with your net profits and then **add**:

☐ any disallowable expenses such as entertaining;
☐ your own salary or money you have taken out of the business;
☐ depreciation;
☐ increases in general provisions for bad debts (you can only deduct specific debts and any increase in general provisions must be added to your profit before calculating tax);
☐ patent royalties and other *charges*;

HOW SMALL AND MEDIUM-SIZED BUSINESSES ARE TAXED

- non-trade debts;
- fines and penalties;
- goods or services taken out of the business for your own or your friends'/family's use (less any price paid).
  You then **deduct** from profits:

- any decrease in general bad debt provisions;
- any charges paid (such as royalty payments) which are included in your personal Income Tax computation.

For details of expenses you can deduct to arrive at profits (allowable expenses) and what proportion of the cost of assets can be claimed (known as capital allowances) see Part 2. Note that capital allowances are now deducted to arrive at your Schedule D Case I taxable profits but these are calculated separately.

So your adjusted profits will look like this:

	[£]	[£]
Net profit (per accounts)		X
Add:		
Your wages	X	
Depreciation	X	
Increases in general debt provisions	X	
Entertaining	X	
Fines	X	
	X	
Adjusted trading profit		X

When you are calculating your Schedule D Case I profits (these are profits from self-employment) you must use the *accruals basis* which means that:

- sales must be accounted for when they take place (usually when invoiced), not when you are paid;
- purchases must be accounted for at the time the debt to the supplier is incurred, not necessarily when you pay for these goods or services.

> **Tax tip:** If your turnover is less than £15,000 you only need to supply a 'three-line account' on your Tax Return comprising turnover, total expenses and profit. You do not need to itemize all the expenses you are claiming.

BASIS OF ASSESSMENT

As detailed above, you are assessed for tax on the profits of your 12-month *accounting period* ended in the tax year. In most cases this will not be the same as the tax year. From 1997/98 onwards all businesses are taxed on this basis. In the past, if your business was started before 6 April 1994 you would have been assessed on your profits in the accounting year ending in the preceding tax year (the *preceding year basis*). If this was the case you would have included two years of accounts on your 1996/97 Tax Return which was the transitional year from the old system to the new.

You may be taxed over a different period if your business is new, has ceased or you have changed your accounting year. In this case some of your profits may be taxed twice. These are known as *overlap* profits.

NEW BUSINESSES

The basic rules are as follows.

New businesses (on commencement)

- *Tax Year 1:* Business is assessed on profits from the date of commencement to the end of the tax year 5 April.
- *Tax Year 2:* If there is an accounting date you are assesed on profits in the:
  – 12 months ending on that date;
  – if this accounting period is less than 12 months, the first 12 months of trading is assessed.
  If there is no accounting date in that tax year, then the business is assessed on the tax year itself.
- *Tax Year 3:* Business is assessed on profits in the accounting year ending in the tax year. (If there is no accounting date in the second year, the basis is 12 months to the accounting date in the third year.)

For example, a business starts on 31 June 1996 and draws up its first accounts on 31 June 1997, 12 months later.

Year 1: (96/97 tax year) basis of assessment:	31 June 1996 to 5 April 1997
Year 2: (97/98 tax year) basis of assessment:	31 June 1996 to 31 June 1997

So profits from 31 June 1996 to 5 April 1997 will be taxed twice – in both year 1 and year 2. These overlap profits can be deducted in the year of cessation of your business or if you change accounting year.

> **Tax tip:** Before starting or ceasing in business and before changing accounting year, seek advice from an accountant to minimize overlap profits and maximize overlap relief.

CHANGING ACCOUNTING YEAR

If you change your accounting year you may also suffer overlap profits, but could also claim overlap relief.

If your new accounting period is less than 12 months, you will be assessed on the 12 months to the new accounting date resulting in overlap profits (profits taxed twice).

If your new accounting period is more than 12 months you may be able to get overlap relief on profits taxed twice when your business started.

If no accounting period ends in that tax year and the accounting period is greater than 12 months, you will be taxed on the 12 months ending on the new accounting date.

> **Tax tip:** If you move your accounting year away from 5 April (a longer accounting year) overlap profits will be created. Moving it closer to 5 April will result in overlap relief. Always ask your accountant for the tax implications of changing your accounting year.

IF YOU MAKE A LOSS

You will see several boxes on your Tax Return covering losses. You can either:

ACCOUNTS AND TAX

- carry forward losses against future profits of the **same** business. Losses must be offset against the first available profits and you must make a claim to carry forward losses within five years of the 31 January following the end of the tax year in which the loss arose;
- offset losses against other income (such as income from employment); or
- carry back losses to earlier years.

> **Tax tips:**
> - Seek advice before deciding what to do with your losses. For instance, if you carry them forward and have insufficient profits in the next year, you will wipe out all your personal allowances (you will no longer benefit from being able to earn a certain amount free of tax).
> - If you are offsetting losses against total income (known as Section 380) there are various ways you can offset the losses with four permutations on year of loss and previous year. You must find the most beneficial way to claim these losses. You have 22 months from the end of the year of loss to make a claim.

Your trading losses can also be offset against your individual Capital Gains Tax liability.

Special rules for new businesses

If you make a loss in the first four tax years of your trade, you can offset these losses against your statutory total income of the three tax years preceding the tax year of loss. So if you were previously an employee these losses can be used to get a tax rebate on tax previously paid as an employee.

> **Tax tip:** Although this is a valuable concession, it may not always be the best alternative.

6

EMPLOYING STAFF

ARE THEY EMPLOYEES OR SELF-EMPLOYED?

This will be the first thing to ascertain. There will be a great advantage to you if they are self-employed. You will not be responsible for deducting PAYE tax and National Insurance and will save on the additional costs of employing staff including desk, telephones, paid holiday, sick pay, expenses, pension scheme, payroll and personnel departments, etc.

However, it is not easy for anyone you employ to be classed as self-employed.
The golden rules for a person to be classed as self-employed are:

- [ ] you pay them for a specific good or service and **not** for their time;
- [ ] they use their own tools or equipment;
- [ ] they incur financial risk (ie they are not guaranteed work and they must invest their own money in staff, stock or equipment needed for the job);
- [ ] they have no rights to pension arrangements, sick pay or holiday pay;
- [ ] they do not work at or from your premises (unless required to provide a service such as mending a computer);
- [ ] they are responsible for correcting unsatisfactory work;
- [ ] they do not work for you for more than 75 per cent of their working time or do not receive more than 75 per cent of their earnings from you;
- [ ] they have the trappings of a business such as a business bank account, business address and accountant.

EMPLOYING STAFF

If someone works for you – even for one day – and you pay them for the time they work (either by the hour or day), you must usually treat them as an employee for tax purposes.

PAYE AND NATIONAL INSURANCE

You must deduct/collect PAYE and National Insurance due up to the fifth day of each month (tax months run from the 6th of one month to the 5th of the next) and pay this to the Collector of Taxes no later than the 19th day of each month.

Note: Payments may be made on a quarterly basis where the average monthly amount of PAYE and NICs is less than £600.

Each employee is given a Tax Code (you should be given notice of this by the Inland Revenue on form P6) and you – or your payroll department or agency – will receive tax tables to calculate how much tax needs to be deducted at each pay date. This ensures that the tax collected at each pay date is the correct proportion of the tax due for the whole year and tax allowances are spread evenly over the whole tax year.

A form P11 deduction working sheet must be filled in for **each** employee at **each** pay date. This will show:

- gross pay for pay period (week/month);
- total gross pay from 6 April to date;
- amount of pay not taxed ('free pay') to date as determined by the Tax Code;
- total taxable pay to date (gross pay less free pay);
- total tax due to date;
- tax to be deducted or refunded;
- National Insurance to be paid – employers and employees.

NEW EMPLOYEES

New employees have to give you form P45 given to them by their previous employer or by the Benefit Office. You should be given Parts 2 and 3. Retain Part 2 to fill in deduction sheets for the new employee and send Part 3 to the Tax Inspector.

If an employee is unable to produce a P45 he must sign a starting-up certificate, form P46. As an employer you must complete the rest of this and send it to the Tax Office.

However, if the employee earns less than the tax and NI thresholds and certifies on form P46 that this job is his only or main employment, the Revenue need not be notified.

Tax must be deducted at the basic rate if the employee does not complete form P46.

WHEN STAFF LEAVE

You must complete form P45 which is a four-part document. It shows the particulars of the employee's Tax Code, gross pay to date and tax paid to date. Part 1 is sent to the Tax Inspector and Parts 1A, 2 and 3 are handed to the leaving employee.

THE FORMS YOU WILL NEED

P6   Notice of employee's Tax Code or amended code sent to the employer by the Tax Inspector.

P9D   End of year return showing expenses payments, benefits in kind, etc of a lower paid employee (earning under £8500 a year including benefits). The deadline for sending this to the Revenue and giving a copy to the employee is 6 July following the end of the tax year.

P11D   Same as above (including the deadlines) but for higher paid employees and directors.

P11   Deduction working sheet you complete to work out weekly/monthly tax and NIC.

P14   End of year summary showing totals of individual's name, final tax code, total pay, total tax and NIC paid during the year, particulars of pay and tax in the previous employment if the employee has joined during the year. This must be submitted by 19 May following the end of the tax year. The form is in three parts with 1 and 2 sent to the Tax Office and DSS. The third is the employee's copy, known as the P60.

P60   Employer's certificate of pay, tax and National Insurance contributions paid, given to each employee by 31 May following the end of the tax year.

P35   Employer's annual return to the Inspector of Taxes giving – in summary form – all employees' Income Tax and NIC payments. The P35 must be submitted by 19 May following the end of the tax year.

P45   Form completed by employer when an employee leaves and given to the employer by new employees when they start work.

WARNING: Failure to make the annual returns required from employers under PAYE (which must be submitted by 19 May following the year of assessment) results in a £100 penalty per month.

SPECIAL RULES FOR THE CONSTRUCTION INDUSTRY

Contractors and labourers must be paid with deduction of basic rate tax at source with this tax paid over to the Inland Revenue even if they are not employees **unless** they hold an exemption certificate. The system is complicated and further changes are to be made although these are not expected before August 1999. As a result all subcontract exemption certificates now have an expiry date of 31 July 1998. The changes are expected to lead to a further dramatic reduction in the numbers of subcontractors who can obtain a tax exemption certificate. If you are a subcontractor or run a construction company you should seek advice from your accountant or Tax Office.

USEFUL CONTACTS

If you are planning to or already employ staff and need help and advice contact The Employer's Helpline on 0345 143143 for both PAYE and NIC enquiries.

7

DEALING WITH THE INLAND REVENUE AND CUSTOMS

INLAND REVENUE

Self assessment has given individual taxpayers the right to calculate their own tax liability, should they want to. But this comes at a price. To ensure that taxpayers do not abuse this to evade tax, the Inland Revenue is undertaking spot checks on a small percentage of taxpayers. One in 33 self-employed will suffer a random check by the Inland Revenue each year, so you cannot rule out an examination of your accounts by a Tax Inspector. Also remember that all Tax Returns will still be checked by the Inland Revenue and if you have claimed an usually high amount of expenses or your profits are unusually low, this could spark further investigation.

Self assessment also requires you to:

- ☐ keep records for five years after the date you send back your Tax Return (or face a fine of up to £3000);
- ☐ send back your Tax Return by 31 January following the end of the tax year (or be fined £100 rising to £60 a day for those who are very late with their returns);
- ☐ pay your tax bill by 31 January following the end of the tax year.

You may have already noticed that you now only have to deal with one Tax Office for your self-employed and personal tax affairs.

TAX INVESTIGATIONS

The self assessment rules gives your Tax Inspector the right to enquire into your tax affairs without giving any reason. If you are to be the subject of an enquiry, you will be given written notice of any enquiry within a year of the end of the quarter in which you sent in your completed return. If you are selected for an enquiry you will be sent information telling you what to expect.

You will usually be given 30 days' notice in which to produce certain documents supporting information given on your Tax Return (although you can appeal against this).

WARNING: If you fail to produce documents your Tax Inspector asks for during an enquiry, you can be fined £50. If you still fail to produce the documents a daily penalty of £30 will be imposed rising to £150 if your inspector takes the case to the Inland Revenue Commissioners.

If you disagree with an assessment you can appeal in writing within 30 days giving grounds of appeal.

You can also appeal to the General Commissioners if you feel an enquiry should not have been undertaken or is being continued unnecessarily.

Once the enquiry has been completed, you will be told this and also told how much tax you owe and possibly that you should amend your self assessment.

These enquiries are normally straightforward and deal with minor points that need clarification.

Only one enquiry can take place into each Tax Return. However, the law does allow a *discovery assessment* if you have been acting fraudulently or negligently but not if you made a simple arithmetic mistake.

Discovery assessments are far more onerous and usually mean your tax inspector has discovered some income or a gain that you have failed to declare or on which you have paid too little tax. If you have disclosed everything required a discovery assessment cannot be made.

Time limits for these inspections are five years from the 31 January following the tax year in question. However, in cases of fraud or negligence the time limit is extended to 20 years.

HOW SMALL AND MEDIUM-SIZED BUSINESSES ARE TAXED

WARNING: You – not your accountant or tax adviser – are responsible for what is included on your Tax Return. As such you are ultimately liable for what is included, for submitting your Tax Return on time and for paying your tax.

There are three types of appeal you can make:

- **The General Commissioners** hear appeals against enquiries into self assessments or discovery assessments issued by a Tax Inspector. The Commissioners are part-time and usually made up of business and professional people.
- **The Special Commissioners** are paid professionals who hear appeals involving more complex points.
- **The Inland Revenue Adjudicator** is the only organization independent of the Inland Revenue. But it only deals with complaints about the way in which the Revenue handles your affairs (delays etc). It cannot deal with appeals against assessments.

> **Tax tip:** To help Tax Inspectors to examine your accounts, the Inland Revenue produces *Business Economic Notes*. Ask if there are any notes covering your type of business as this will give you an insight into what the Tax Inspector expects from your business. The Inland Revenue knows roughly what profit most types of business make as a percentage of turnover so if your profit is exceptionally low, it may seek an explanation.

PAYING TAX

The self-employed have three tax payment dates:

- 31 January during the tax year for the first payment 'on account';
- 31 July following the end of the tax year for the second payment on account;
- 31 January following the end of the tax year for any balancing payments.

Your payments on account are normally half the total income tax liability (less any tax deducted at source) for the previous tax year. The balance of any tax liability plus the whole of your Capital Gains Tax liability is then due on the 31 January following these two interim payments.

> **Tax tip:** Your payments on account are now assessed on your Tax Return (see Question 18 on page 7). If you think your payments on account will be lower in the 1998/99 tax year because your profits will be reduced, you can make a claim to reduce your payments. However, do not do this to save on advance tax payments. If you fraudulently or negligently ask for a reduction in your payments on account you will be fined.

If your profits are likely to be higher than in the preceding year, you do not have to increase your interim payments.

Interest on late payment/overpayment

You will be charged interest on late payment of tax. If you miss the 31 January final tax payment deadline by 28 days you will be surcharged 5 per cent of tax owed rising to 10 per cent if your tax is still unpaid more than six months after this deadline.

In addition you will be charged interest from the date you should have made your payments on account and the balancing payment.

> **Tax tip:** If you have paid too much tax because you have been sent a wrong assessment (not through your own fault) you can ask the Inland Revenue to pay you interest.

CUSTOMS

Local VAT offices are responsible for providing advice to businesses in their area. Completed VAT returns must be sent to the VAT Central Unit at Southend.

You should expect to be visited by an officer from the local VAT office from time to time. These visits are to ensure that VAT is being applied properly. You must be prepared for these inspections and make sure that your record-keeping and paperwork are in order.

If you are unhappy with any decision as to the application of VAT you can ask your local VAT office to reconsider before making a formal appeal.

ASSESSMENTS

If Customs think you have failed to make accurate returns or these are incomplete, you will be sent a VAT assessment of the amount they

HOW SMALL AND MEDIUM-SIZED BUSINESSES ARE TAXED

believe you owe. The time limit for making assessments is normally six years after the end of the accounting period covered. However, in the case of fraud, dishonest conduct and the issuing of unauthorised tax invoices, this time limit is extended to 20 years.

The VAT tribunals are independent of Customs and you can appeal provided you have made VAT returns and payments. You must lodge your appeal with the tribunal within 30 days of the date of any Customs decision you wish to dispute.

WARNING: If you deliberately evade tax this amounts to criminal fraud. The penalty in a magistrates' court (summary conviction) has a maximum prison term of six months and a fine of either £2000 or three times the tax involved whichever is the greater. If you are convicted by a jury the maximum prison term is seven years and fines are unlimited.

Even simple mistakes – not deliberate fraud – can result in fines and penalties.

- Late notification of registration results in a penalty which is the greater of:
  – £50; and
  – a percentage of net tax due from the date when registration should have taken place ranging from 5 to 15 per cent depending on the delay.
- Civil fraud, where you take steps or omit to take steps, in order to evade tax results in a penalty of 100 per cent of the tax involved.
- Unauthorized issue of VAT invoices by those not registered results in a 15 per cent penalty of the VAT involved.
- Breaches of regulations such as failure to keep proper accounting records range in fines of £5 to £15 per day with a minimum penalty of £50. If the breach is non-payment or failure to make returns on time, the daily penalty is a percentage of the tax involved if this is greater ranging from $1/6$ per cent to $1/2$ per cent.
- Failure to preserve records for the required period gives rise to a fixed fine of £500.
- Late submission of VAT returns or late payment results in a surcharge liability notice
- Misdeclarations result in a penalty of 15 per cent of the tax involved.
- Interest is also charged on VAT subject to an assessment and this is not deductible from taxable profits.

DEALING WITH THE INLAND REVENUE AND CUSTOMS

There is a myriad of fines and penalties, so you should be aware of all the requirements and avoid them.

One point worth noting is that mitigation is allowed for some penalties and some do not apply if you have a reasonable excuse. But not having sufficient funds to pay your VAT or the fact that you relied on someone else to pay it or file your returns, are not reasonable excuses. What amounts to a 'reasonable excuse' and 'mitigating circumstances' is not clearly defined. However, co-operation and full disclosure are usually grounds for mitigation.

PART 2:
WAYS TO SAVE TAX

8

MAKING SURE YOU CLAIM THE MAXIMUM EXPENSES

Claiming every expense allowable is one of the easiest ways to reduce your profits and therefore your tax bill.

Generally you can only deduct expenses that are incurred *wholly and exclusively* for business purposes. Employees must also show that these expenses are *necessarily* incurred. So as a self-employed person you have more freedom to deduct expenses from your income to reduce your profits – and in turn your tax bill. You do not have to prove that the expenses were necessary and there are even exceptions to the wholly and exclusively rule. For instance, you do not have to use your car wholly and exclusively for business, and can claim the *business proportion* of any expenses.

Basically you can **deduct most expenses and expenditure which form part of your day-to-day running costs, apart from:**

- [ ] items of capital expenditure (the purchase of assets, equipment, tools, cars, furniture, etc) and the costs of acquiring them – these are deducted as Capital allowances not as business expenses;
- [ ] your own salary;
- [ ] the cost of entertaining (other than staff);
- [ ] anything that is covered by another tax provision (such as deeds of covenant);
- [ ] depreciation (the loss in value) of assets;
- [ ] anything you buy for personal use/bought for domestic use;
- [ ] fines and penalties for late payment of tax or VAT.

So the list of possible expenses is almost endless. The items in Table 8.1 include those you may have overlooked or are unsure about, but remember this is a checklist – not a comprehensive summary.

WAYS TO SAVE TAX

Table 8.1 *Overview of what you can and cannot deduct*

What you can deduct	What you cannot
Legal fees for debt collection and preparing trading contracts and employee service contracts.	Half your Class 4 National Insurance payments (this has now been withdrawn with 1995/96 the last year you could claim this as an expense).
Hire purchase payments and leasing rent for cars and machinery.	Parking fines (although you can pay these for employees) or the cost of defending yourself against a criminal charge in a court case from an offence (such as a drink-drive ban).
Car hire – providing the costs are reasonable (you cannot hire a Ferrari!).	Political and charitable donations (other than to a small local charity).
The running costs of your own car or a proportion relating to the amount of business usage – you can deduct a proportion of your motoring insurance, car tax, maintenance and fuel.	You cannot deduct your own life insurance, personal accident insurance, permanent health insurance and private medical insurance (but you can if you provide it for your employees).
Bank charges, loan interest and overdraft fees on business accounts (that is why it is advisable to have a separate business account) but not the repayment of loans.	You cannot deduct the costs of alterations, improvements or additions to your business premises.
Interest on loans from friends and relatives who have helped you start your business (providing they do not have a say in how the company is run and the loan should be covered by a written agreement).	You cannot claim for anything which has a dual purpose – business and pleasure such as a holiday combined with business or if you use your car for a trip which is part leisure or part business.
Credit card charges.	Your tax bills.
If you work from home you can claim a proportion of the costs of running your home as a business expense – but only the proportion that relates to your business, including a proportion of mortgage interest/rent, cleaning, fuel and light, etc. If you use one room out of six as an office, you can deduct a sixth of these bills.	Pre-trading expenses – for instance, if you spent money on rent and rates on your business premises before you started trading you can deduct these but not as expenses if your business was set up before 6 April 1995. These come under losses. Note these expenses can be incurred up to seven years before your business actually starts/started.
Accountancy and audit fees.	Money taken out of your business to repay a loan.
Telephone bills, including line rental, and line installation can also be deducted. Again if your phone is also your private phone you can only claim the business proportion and a share of the rental. Itemized calls make the calculation more accurate.	If you are an employee you can claim expenses from your employer for entertaining clients and this will not be taxable. But if you are self-employed **you cannot claim for entertaining** and hospitality – even if it is useful to help boost the sales of your business
Clothing you need for work, eg overalls or protective clothing.	You cannot normally deduct everyday clothing even if you bought it for business use.
VAT – if you are not registered for VAT you can still claim it back by including it in the cost of any items of allowable expenditure.	Furniture, computers, filing cabinets – these are not business expenses and must be claimed under capital allowances however small items of equipment – for instance filing trays – may be included in business expenses.
If you have to pay insurance to cover business equipment you can deduct this or you can claim a proportion of your household insurance bills if you work from home.	Travel between home and your place of work.
Wages if you employ your wife or husband – but you must show that work is actually done and that the wage is at the market rate.	

CLAIM THE MAXIMUM EXPENSES

Tax warning: Many businesses fall into the trap of spending too much on entertaining. It is disallowable as an expense, except when you are entertaining your own staff in which case it is tax deductible. However, if you spend more than £75 this could be a P11D (taxable business expense) item for staff.

Tax tips:

- You can deduct the cost of expenses you have incurred but **not** yet paid for.
- If you make a payment that covers an expense for more than one accounting period you can deduct the amount that relates to the new year. So if you paid 12 months' rent or a 12-month service contract in advance, only deduct the proportion that relates to the accounting period on your Tax Return.
- If your business takes you away from home, the cost of overnight accommodation in hotels is normally allowed. And if your trade is carried on abroad and you are overseas for at least 60 consecutive days, the travelling costs of your spouse and minor children are also allowed. They can have up to a maximum of two visits per fiscal year.
- Any subscriptions to trade bodies or journals connected with your trade can be deducted as an expense as can any reference books and other specialist literature.

CAPITAL EXPENDITURE VS EXPENSES

As explained in Part 1, the two main deductions you can make from profits to reduce your tax bill are *expenses* and *capital allowances*.

Tax tip: Whenever possible try to make sure items of expenditure are classed as expenses rather than capital allowances. This is because you can deduct 100 per cent of the costs if an item is classed as an expense, but only 25 per cent if it is classed as a capital allowance other than from 2 July 1997 to 1 July 1998 when an increased first-year allowance of 50 per cent has been given to purchases of plant and machinery (but not cars) by small and medium-sized businesses. This has been extended from 2 July 1998 to 1 July 1999, with a first year allowance of 40 per cent. Small and medium-sized business are those with fewer than 250 staff, turnover of not more than £11.2 million and assets not more than £5.6 million..

The distinction between what is capital and what is an expense is not always clear. For example the following items of expenditure can be split into either category.

- **Advertising**: The cost can be deducted as expenditure but fixed signs are classed as capital.
- **Removals**: The costs can only be deducted as an expense if the move was not an expansionary one (you did not move to bigger premises).
- **Repairs**: If you are repairing or replacing a subsidiary part of an asset this is an expense, but replacing all or nearly all of the asset is classed as capital expenditure. Initial repairs to remedy a previous owner's wear and tear are only allowed as an expense if the asset was in a useable condition. If you needed to make repairs before the asset could be used, this is capital expenditure.

WHAT YOU CAN CLAIM AS EXPENSES

Legal, accounting and professional fees

You can claim:

- accountancy charges;
- legal costs for renewing a short lease of 50 years or less (but not any fees for renegotiation of the lease);
- legal and other professional fees for drafting employee contracts;
- costs incurred in collecting trade debts;
- fees for defending your rights to an asset (known as title to fixed assets);
- you can also deduct damages paid.

You cannot claim:

- fees incurred in renegotiating or purchasing long leases/buying property (these are included with other costs when calculating capital allowances);
- fees for settling your own tax liabilities/back duty;
- fees for setting up your business;
- fees for drafting partnership agreements (these are classed as personal not business agreements);

CLAIM THE MAXIMUM EXPENSES

- legal fees defending breaches of the law, for instance, legal fees for defending you in a drink-drive ban.

Financing costs

You can claim:

- interest paid to a bank/building society for trade purposes;
- credit card interest and fees;
- hire purchase interest;
- leasing payments;
- the incidental costs of obtaining loan finance.

You cannot claim:

- interest on money borrowed to set up your business;
- the part of a loan repayment which is a capital repayment;
- interest on overdue tax.

> **Tax tip:** Because you can claim interest on loans to purchase equipment, you may be better off buying your assets with a loan or on hire purchase. That way you do not tie up capital and in turn this capital can be used to invest in other aspects of your business.

Employee costs

You can claim:

- salaries, bonuses, etc paid to staff with the additional costs such as National Insurance contributions and insurance benefits;
- the cost of fees paid to subcontractors or the hiring of locums to stand in for you;
- costs of entertaining staff (such as the Christmas party);
- redundancy payments – redundancy pay in excess of the statutory amount is also allowed where the trade ceases (the total limit is four times the statutory amount);
- contributions to an approved pension fund;
- payments for technical education and training of staff.

You cannot claim:

- your own wages, tax or National Insurance or pension costs

(although you do get tax relief on this);
- [ ] any money you take out of the business.

> **Tax tip:** Employ your spouse or other members of your family and you can then deduct their wages as an expense. But remember payments must not be excessive and must be for work actually done.

VAT

If you are **not** registered for VAT either because your trade is exempt, partly exempt or your turnover is below the VAT threshold, you can reclaim VAT added to expenses and capital items by including it in the price paid.

But if you are registered for VAT, you must exclude it when claiming expenses and deal with Customs.

Bad debts

You can only claim for:

- [ ] bad debts actually written off.

You cannot claim for:

- [ ] any movement in general provisions.

Travelling

You can claim for:

- [ ] the cost of running your car (or a proportion if also used privately) including insurance, servicing, road tax, repairs, parking fees, fuel and breakdown cover;
- [ ] hiring and leasing charges (or business proportion of these);
- [ ] rail, air fares, taxis, etc;
- [ ] hotels while travelling on business (but not the cost of lunches).

You cannot claim for:

- [ ] travelling from home to your place of business unless you are an itinerant trader and although you do not work at home it is your base;

- [ ] the cost of buying a car (this comes under capital allowances);
- [ ] car hire charges may be restricted and cannot be excessive.

Leasing or buying cars

If you purchase a car for more than £12,000, you can only claim a maximum of £3000 as a capital allowance. So you will not be able to write down the maximum 25 per cent allowed. The other option may be to hire or lease your cars. But there is also a restriction on annual hire and finances charges as follows:

$$\frac{£12,000 + 1/2 \text{ (Retail price - £12,000)}}{\text{Retail price}} \times \begin{array}{l}\text{Annual rental (or} \\ \text{Depreciation + Interest)}\end{array}$$

So, if you rent a car for £2000 a year and it cost £16,000 the calculation would be:

$$\frac{£12,000 + 1/2 \text{ (£16,000 - £12,000)}}{£16,000} = 0.875\% \times £2000 = £1750$$

As £2000 (all the rent) will have been deducted in your trading accounts £2000 - £1750 = £250 will be **disallowed** in computing taxable profits. This effectively means you can only deduct £1750 as a trading expense (note rents and operating leases are deducted as expenses not capital allowances).

Note: If the contract was entered into before 11 March 1992, £8000 replaces the £12,000.

However, if you are buying the car on an **HP** agreement or lease with an option to purchase, you can deduct **all** the annual interest as a trade expense **providing** you do not pay more than 1 per cent of the car's retail price (when new) when exercising the option to purchase. **And** you can claim *capital allowances* on the cash price when the agreement begins. This is because for tax the car is treated as if purchased outright.

Computers

You can claim:

You cannot claim:

- hardware (this must be claimed as a capital allowance); or
- software if bought as a package with hardware.

Education and enterprise

You can claim for:

- your own training/education courses provided they are to update existing knowledge or skills;
- staff training;
- contributions to training and enterprise councils or business link organizations;
- contributions to an approved local enterprise agency.

You cannot claim for:

- education/training so that you can acquire new knowledge or skills.

Business premises

Again some items may be claimed as expenses and others as capital allowances.

Dedicated business premises
You can claim as an expense:

- all rent;
- business rates;
- water rates;
- costs of lighting;
- costs of heating;
- power;
- insurance;
- cleaning;
- security etc.

If you work from home
You can claim a proportion of your home expenses. This is usually

worked out on a room basis. So if you have four rooms (excluding kitchens and bathrooms) and work in one room you can deduct a quarter of your household expenses.

Note: If you use a room exclusively for business you may be liable to Capital Gains Tax on sale of the property.

Expenses you can claim a proportion of include:

- mortgage interest – but not repayments.
  Note: A recent concession by the Inland Revenue allows you to claim mortgage interest relief (MIRAS) on the proportion of the loan to buy your home and interest attributed to the business use can be deducted from your profits.
- rent;
- council tax;
- cleaning and maintenance;
- heating, lighting and power.

You cannot claim:

- anything that is classed as plant or machinery (from office furniture to computers) as this must be claimed as a capital allowance.

Renting, buying or leasing business premises

When deciding on your business premises you should consider the tax implications.

The advantage of renting is that you can claim all the costs as a business expense. However, many businesses will be required to take out a lease.

The taxation of leases depends on whether they are classed as short or long leases. Short leases do not exceed 50 years. The premium on a long lease is classed as capital.

With a short lease, the amount the landlord is taxed on as rent (under Schedule A) is deductible as an expense by the lessee. But this must be spread over the term of the lease less one year.

As this is a complex calculation it is easier to show an example.

Business A takes over the lease of a business premises.

Premium: £80,000
Rent: £20,000 per annum
Term of lease: 21 years

To find out how much the landlord is taxed on as rent:

Total premium payable £80,000

Less: Discount (rent spread over term) taxed as capital:

21 years − 1 year (the first is disallowable) × 2% (set rate) = 40%
So deduct 40% of £80,000 = (32,000)

Assessable to landlord as additional rent £48,000

So Business A can claim: £48,000 = £2286
              21 (full term of lease)
Plus rent of £20,000
                              £22,286

a year as an expense for the business premises.

If you are purchasing premises note that capital allowances are **only** given on agricultural buildings and industrial buildings (factories, warehouses, hotels and buildings in enterprise zones) but **not** retail shops, offices, showrooms or other business premises. If you are purchasing an industrial building the tax life of the building and any periods of non-usage affect your tax position so seek advice from an accountant.

Because of these restrictions you should be aware of what constitutes a building and what qualifies as plant. The general rules are that if it is apparatus **with** which the business is carried on it is plant. But if it is **in** which the business is carried on it is classed as or part of a building. So movable office partitions are plant but not fixed partitions, but a false ceiling to hide pipes is classed as part of the building not as plant. Items that are classed as part of the building cannot be deducted as a capital allowance. However, Revenue practice and past cases have led to some exceptions, which can be treated as plant and therefore qualify for capital allowances, including:

- burglar alarm systems;
- advertising hoardings, signs and displays;
- electrical, gas and sewerage systems installed to meet the particular requirements of the business or to serve particular machinery or plant (such as electrical cables for computers);
- ventilation, air conditioning and water heating systems and any ceilings or floors used to house these;
- counters, checkouts, storage equipment including cold rooms;
- washbasins, sinks, cookers, etc.

Notes: Repairs to premises and machinery are normally allowed as an expense but any

- alterations or improvements must be claimed as a capital allowance.
- The legal, surveying and other professional costs involved in buying premises are treated as part of their cost and as such are claimed as capital allowances (not expense).

Allowable expenses you may not have considered

- **Gifts**: Provided they carry a prominent advertisement (your company name on a diary or pen), do not exceed £10 per person per annum and are not food, tobacco or drink.

- **Charitable donations**: These can also help promote your business if your donation is published or publicized. However, you can only make small donations to local charities.

9

DEDUCTING CAPITAL EXPENSES

WHAT CAN BE CLAIMED AS A CAPITAL ALLOWANCE

Major purchases are **not** deducted as business expenses. If you buy a computer or machinery this is not an *allowable business expense*. It is classed as capital expenditure and as such it should be deducted as a capital allowance. Your capital allowances are then deducted from your turnover along with your allowable business expenses to give your taxable profit.

You can deduct all of your *allowable business expenses* but only a proportion of your capital expenditure, your *capital allowance*.

> **Tax tips:**
>
> ☐ First year capital allowances have been increased for small and medium-sized businesses until 1 July 1999. Read the rules later in the chapter for ways to save tax.
> ☐ Because of the way capital allowances work, it may be more tax efficient to lease an item of equipment as you can claim all of the leasing costs as a business expense but only 25 per cent as a capital allowance.

Capital allowances are given on items of equipment or capital assets:

☐ plant and machinery – including machines and computers, furniture, ladders and scaffolding, tools and equipment, vans and lorries (include computer software only if you buy this as part of your computer package);

DEDUCTING CAPITAL EXPENSES

- cars;
- industrial buildings – if you run a factory, the cost (but not rents);
- fixtures and fittings;
- agricultural buildings; and
- certain other items including mineral extraction, dredging, scientific research, patents, and know-how.

You can only get capital allowances on items used *wholly and exclusively* for the business and which belong to the business. But as with allowable expenses there are exceptions – you can claim a proportion of the costs of cars that are for part business and part private use.

Industrial buildings can only be those that are used for making goods for resale, processing materials or storing goods and materials used in manufacturing and processing. You cannot claim for the cost of your home even if you use part of it for business. And you cannot claim for retail shops, showrooms or offices – these do not qualify for capital allowances.

If you are running a hotel you can qualify for an allowance if the hotel is open for at least four months in the season between April and October, has at least ten letting bedrooms and you provide extra services including breakfast and dinner, making beds and cleaning rooms. You can also claim for the cost of building extensions to hotels of ten bedrooms or more.

You cannot claim for the cost of land even if it is used for your business and you cannot claim for anything you have bought solely for private use.

If you are **not** registered for VAT you should include the VAT element of the price you pay for capital assets. This is a way for you to claim it back. However, if you are VAT-registered you should not include the VAT element and must include this on your VAT return instead.

Capital allowances cover those items that have a useful life of more than two or three years. So spending on computer software may be an allowable business expense (100 per cent tax deductible) rather than a capital allowance (unless you buy the software as a package with your computer).

HOW TO WORK OUT YOUR CAPITAL ALLOWANCES

For plant and machinery, computers, etc you can claim up to **25 per cent** of the cost in the year in which you buy it. (But see first year allowances on page 80 for extra allowances). The rest is written off over a number of years at up to 25 per cent of the remaining value. For example:

> You spend **£3000** on a computer:
>
> In the year you bought it you can deduct 25 per cent as a capital allowance = **£750.**
>
> It now has a *written-down* value of £3000 - £750 = **£2250**
>
> In the second year you can claim a capital allowance of 25 per cent on this written-down value of £2250:
>
> 25% of £2250 = **£562.50**
>
> The written down value is now £2250 - £562.50 = **£1687.50.**
>
> You continue writing down your capital until it is completely written off.

When you sell your asset a separate calculation must be made. The sale proceeds (limited to a maximum of the original cost) are deducted from your 'pool' of capital expenditure.

SELLING BUSINESS ASSETS AT A PROFIT

The balancing charge is designed to cover any profit you may make where the sale proceeds exceed the written down value of your pool. The balancing charge is **added** to your profits when calculating how much tax you owe (so you do not calculate a 25 per cent allowance). Balancing allowances are deducted from profits, when you sell an item at a loss (for less than the written-down value) when your trade ceases or if you sell assets not wholly used for business purposes, cars or short-life assets. Otherwise they are used to reduce the 'pool' of capital assets.

> If you bought six items of machinery for £20,000 in total
> You then have a pool value of £20,000
> And you claimed capital allowances (amount you can offset against tax) of:
>
> ☐ Year 1, 25% of £20,000 = **£5000**
>   ☐ Written-down value or value of the pool £20,000 - £5000 = £15,000
>   Year 2, 25% of £15,000 = **£3750**
>   ☐ Written-down value £15,000 - £3750 = £11,250
>   Year 3, 25% of £11,250 = **£2812.50**
>   ☐ Written-down value £11,250 - £2812.50 = £8437.50
>
> Assume the business ceases to trade and the machinery is then sold for £10,000 (more than the written-down value) you would face a *balancing charge* of:
>
> £10,000 - £8437.50 = **£1562.50** added to your profits
>
> If the machinery was sold for £5000 (less than the written-down value) you would get a *balancing allowance* covering your loss:
>
> £5000 - £8437.50 = **-£3437.50**

POOLING ASSETS

To make things more simple you can put all your plant and machinery into a *pool of expenditure* so you do not have to calculate each item separately. So for the 1996–97 Tax Return you will take the written-down value of capital assets at the end of your last accounting period (or the last accounting period in which you paid tax) and add in any new items you have purchased to create a pool.

So if your written-down value was £8000 and you have bought £4000 of capital assets your total *pool value* will be £8000 + £4000 = £12,000. The pool means you only have to work out 25 per cent of £12,000 – not 25 per cent of each individual asset – to claim your capital allowance.

However, some items cannot be included in a pool. Cars, but not lorries and vans, must be calculated separately or in their own pool if you have purchased more than one. The maximum you can write down in any year is £3000. Cars which cost more than £12,000 cannot be included in this pool and must be calculated separately as must **cars used partly for private motoring**.

The capital allowance on industrial and other buildings must also be calculated separately.

FIRST-YEAR ALLOWANCES

For expenditure on plant and machinery (but not cars, long-life assets or items for lease or hire) between 2 July 1997 and 1 July 1998, a higher first-year allowance of 50 per cent has been introduced for small and medium-sized businesses. From 1 July 1998 the rate becomes 40 per cent.

These are businesses which satisfy two of the following conditions:

- turnover not exceeding £11.2 million;
- assets not exceeding £5.6 million;
- not more than 250 staff.

Note: First-year allowances must be calculated separately.

After you have claimed the first-year allowance, the asset then enters the pool. In this case that will be £1250 (£2500 - £1250 capital allowance already claimed).

Tax warning: First-year allowances are a major tax concession. However, because first-year allowances are calculated separately from the general pool, it may not always pay to claim them.

For example:

Assuming first-year allowance not available:		Capital allowance
Pool carried forward	£4000	
Additions	£2500	
Sales proceeds	(£6000)	
	£500	
Capital allowance @ 25%		£125
Assuming 50 per cent first-year allowance		
Pool carried forward	£4000	
Sales proceeds	(£6000)	
	(£2000)	
Balancing charge		(£2000)
Less: First-year allowance		
£2500 @ 50%		£1250
Balancing charge		(£750) added to profits

So by claiming a first-year allowance, the business has lost out.

INDUSTRIAL AND OTHER BUILDINGS

Industrial and other buildings can only be written down at the rate of 4 per cent a year and when you sell the building you will be charged a balancing charge of the difference between the price you sold the building for and its written-down value. So if you sell the building for £25,000 and its written-down value is £20,000, you will have a balancing charge of £5000. This is so you cannot make a profit out of writing down the value of your investment. But if you sell for less than your written-down value you can claim your 'loss' as a balancing allowance. After 25 years there is no need to calculate a balancing allowance or balancing charge.

LONG-LIFE ASSETS

Assets with a working life of 25 years or more (if bought on or after 26 November 1996) now have a written-down rate of 6 per cent instead of 25 per cent. However, this will not apply where a company spends £100,000 or less in any year on such long-life assets.

SHORT-LIFE ASSETS:

If your assets have an expected life of less than five years you can write off the value of the equipment when you get rid of it (its remaining written-down value). But you will have to calculate these *short-life assets* separately from the pool and if you do not get rid of the item within five years you will have to add the balance to the main pool.

You must elect for items to be treated as short-life assets within 12 months of the 31 January following the year of assessment in which the expenditure was made. So, items bought in an accounting year ending 30 September 1997 can be de-pooled by electing before 31 January 2000. The election should be made for assets likely to be sold within four years for less than their written value. You cannot elect for cars to be treated as short-life assets.

APPORTIONING ALLOWANCES

When you buy an item of plant or machinery it does not matter at what point during the year you make the purchase. Even if you buy it the day before the end of your accounting year, you can claim the full capital allowance for that accounting year.

However, if you have an accounting period of more or less than 12 months you cannot claim a full year's capital allowances. You must increase or reduce them proportionately. The calculation will be as follows:

Number of months in business accounting period divided by 12 × 25% of the written-down value

So if you start your business and spend £20,000 on capital assets but your first accounting period is only six months, you can only claim:
6/12 × 25% of £20,000 = £2500

If your business ceases and you sell any items, simply deduct the amount you receive (or their value if you decide to keep them) from the pool. If you sell them for more than the value of the pool you will have a balancing charge. Any remaining value in the pool is not calculated as a capital allowance (you do not claim 25 per cent of its value). Simply deduct the entire sum as a balancing allowance.

Tax tips:

- If you want to delay claiming a capital allowance (for instance until your next accounting year), you can arrange a purchase contract that does not require you to pay for the item for several months as you are not entitled to capital allowances until payment is made. The date you actually pay for your asset – or are obliged to pay for it – is the date you take when calculating capital allowances.
- If you buy equipment for private use (such as a computer) and then use it in your business, you can claim a capital allowance on its market value at the time you start using it for business.
- If you buy on hire purchase, you can claim capital allowances on the original cost of the item cash price. The extra amount you pay in interest or other charges can be claimed as a business expense.

PART 3:
FILLING IN YOUR TAX RETURN

10

THE QUESTIONNAIRE

Read the cover to make sure you fully understand what is required and that the information is correct.

Check that your title, name and address are correct. If they are wrong, simply amend any errors by deleting the information that is wrong and writing the correct information next to it.

Note your Tax Reference as you will need to refer to it in all correspondence with the Inland Revenue.

Note your Tax Office telephone number. This will be useful if you have any questions.

Read carefully through the instructions and note the deadlines for submitting your completed Tax Return.

Everyone has to fill in page 2 to make sure they have the right supplementary pages.

STEP 1: FILL IN THE QUESTIONNAIRE

Read the notes carefully to make sure you do not tick any wrong boxes. For example, you may normally be self-employed but some of your earnings could be classed as earnings from employment because you were employed as a casual worker or an agency arranged work for you. You will know if you were an 'employee' as tax should have been deducted from your pay before you received it.

Q1: EMPLOYMENT

If you are normally self-employed, some earnings may be still classed as earnings from employment if one or more of the following applies:

☐ you were paid for your time, not for providing goods or services;

FILLING IN YOUR TAX RETURN

- ☐ you worked from the premises of someone who you were working for or used their equipment;
- ☐ you earn most (generally more than 75 per cent) of your earnings from one source.

Remember if you had any earnings from employment during the tax year from 6 April 1997 to 5 April 1998 you must tick the *YES* box.

Q2: SHARE SCHEMES

As you have to be a director or employee to benefit from share options, this question will probably not apply.

Q3: SELF-EMPLOYMENT

Tick the *YES* box and make sure you have the appropriate additional pages (colour coded orange).

Q4: PARTNERSHIP

If you were not a sole trader but are in partnership or were at any time during the tax year from 6 April 1997 to 5 April 1998 tick the *YES* box.

Q5: LAND AND PROPERTY

Some income from land and property does **not** have to be included in this section.

- ⇨ If you run a bed and breakfast business or rent out rooms and provide extra services such as meals in your only or main home, your activities will amount to a trade and as such you should tick the *NO* box. These come under self-employment.
- ⇨ Even if you are making the most of the Rent a Room relief – which allows you to rent a room in your home for up to £4250 a year and get that income tax free – you should tick the *YES* box.
- ⇨ If you receive rent from letting out your overseas holiday home this is covered in the foreign income section.

Q6: FOREIGN

This includes any overseas pensions or benefits, income from foreign companies or savings institutions, offshore funds or overseas trusts, rents from land and property, foreign life insurance policies and annuities.

⇨ If you invest in a UK unit trust or investment trust that in turn invests in overseas companies, this is **not** classed as foreign earnings.
⇨ Tick the *YES* box if you want to claim relief for foreign tax that has been deducted on any income or gains – this includes tax deducted on overseas earnings if you are *self-employed*.

Q7: TRUSTS

The *YES* box must be ticked if you were a beneficiary or received money from a trust fund or you created (were the settlor) of a trust. But if you received a legacy in trust (from the estate of a deceased persons) tick the *NO* box.

⇨ If you receive income from a 'nominee' account which is also known as a bare trust do not include this here. For tax purposes the income and profits belong to the beneficiary and not to the trust. Include this income on the relevant pages of your main Tax Return – so shares in a 'nominee' account should be included in the investment section.

Q8: CAPITAL GAINS

See Part 1, Chapter 2 of this book for an explanation of Capital Gains Tax and whether or not you are liable. Note that Capital Gains Tax taxes the profits (gains) you make when you sell investments, businesses or other assets.

Did you sell your home?

Your only or main home is usually exempt from Capital Gains Tax. But if you sold your home during the tax year you must still tick the

YES box. This does **not** mean that you have to pay Capital Gains Tax or that you have to fill in the Capital Gains form. You may only have to do this if you sold some land adjoining your home for development, sold part of your property, rented it out or used your home for running a business. Even in these cases you may be able to escape Capital Gains Tax.

Read Part 1 of this book for an explanation of chargeable assets and chargeable gains.

Q9: NON-RESIDENCE

This will apply to you if you live abroad or lived most of the tax year in another country. If you have not lived or worked overseas tick the *NO* box.

⇨ If you spend less than 183 days in the UK in any tax year and, over four years, an average of less than 91 days, or have spent the entire year overseas you are non-resident.
⇨ If you are living in the UK but come from overseas, tick the *YES* box.

STEP 2: FILL IN THE SUPPLEMENTARY PAGES

Only fill in those pages that you have ticked YES in boxes **Q1** to **Q9**. If you ticked a box – for example self-employment – but do not have the right supplementary pages then ring the Orderline on 0645 000 404 and ask for any missing forms.

As readers of this book will have to fill in the Self-employment pages, these are covered next. You are strongly advised to fill in the supplementary pages **before** filling in the rest of the main eight pages of your Tax Return. If you do not you may not be able to fill in these pages correctly.

Once you have filled in all your supplementary pages tick the *Step 2* box on page 2 of your Tax Return.

STEP 3: FILL IN THE MAIN TAX RETURN

REMEMBER: The Tax Return states 'ignore pence'. This

simply means that you can round all income figures down. For instance, instead of writing £109.55 you simply write £109. Do not round up to £110 unless it works to your advantage – so round up your outgoings.

11

SELF-EMPLOYMENT

📄 PAPERWORK REQUIRED

One copy of the Self-employment pages for each set of business accounts (unless your turnover is less than £15,000). These are the accounts drawn up at the end of your accounting year. If you don't have formal accounts drawn up, you will need records of income and expenditure.

If you pay tax 'on account' (in two instalments) you should have been sent a 'Self Assessment – Statement of Account' form – a tax bill sent for payment by 31 January 1998. You will need this, and the notice of the second instalment in July, to calculate how much tax you still owe for the 1997/98 tax year.

Notes

☐ This chapter refers to your business. You may not consider yourself to be 'in business' because your earnings are low, occasional or in addition to earnings from employment. But from the point of view of the Inland Revenue, you are 'in business'.

☐ The Inland Revenue has special rules to help those whose profits are irregular and may have self-employed earnings one year and none the next. If you are an author or artist, a farmer or market gardener or a foster carer or adult carer ask the Inland Revenue for the special rules that will help you to even out your tax bill.

Only if you receive very isolated payments from self-employment can you avoid filling in the self-employment pages. If this is the case you can put these additional earnings in the 'Other Income' box on page 4 of your Tax Return.

SELF-EMPLOYMENT

WHAT YOU NEED TO KNOW TO FILL IN THESE PAGES

Your *accounting date* is the date up to which you draw up your accounts. It is the end of your *accounting year*, which is usually a 12-month period. If you only have a small amount of self-employment or freelance earnings you may have simply opted to be taxed over the same period as the tax year itself – from 6 April to 5 April. This is known as being taxed on an *actual basis*.

The *accounting year* you must use is the one ending in the 1997/98 tax year. So if your accounting year ends on 5 May 1997 you will include profits for the 12 months to 5 May 1997 on your 1997/98 Tax Return – and then pay this tax by 31 January 1999. Please note that all the self-employed are now taxed on a current year basis. Under the old *preceding year* basis you were taxed on your accounting year ending in the previous tax year.

Special rules for those with new businesses or who closed a business during the tax year

When you set up in business or close a business you are not necessarily taxed on your accounting year. Read the Tax Guidance notes and Part 1, Chapter 5 of this book to find out over what period you will be taxed. These rules mean you could be taxed on the same profits twice – these are known as *overlap profits*. You can claim these back when your business ceases to trade or, in some cases, if you change your accounting year.

> **Tax tips:**
> - ☐ If you have made a loss during the first four tax years of your business, you can offset the loss against income (including salary) you earned in the three tax years before the year in which the loss was made.
> - ☐ If you spent money on setting up your business before you actually started trading you can also claim pre-trading expenses. So money you spend on rent and rates or business equipment can be tax deducted from your business profits after you start trading. The expenses can be incurred up to seven years before your business actually starts.

FILLING IN YOUR TAX RETURN

IF YOU DO NOT HAVE ACCOUNTS DRAWN UP

You no longer need to send your statement of accounts in with your Tax Return. However, you will still need to have accounts to fill in your Tax Return. So it may pay you to employ an accountant to do this – **accountancy fees are tax deductible**.

However, you can draw up your own accounts if your turnover is low, you don't employ a large staff and you know what is required – your accounts must meet accepted accountancy standards.

Remember your turnover should include the value of sales you have made in the accounting year including invoices you have sent out for services provided – even if you have not yet been paid.

You don't need to have a balance sheet to fill in your Tax Return but if your business involves keeping stock you may find this useful.

HOW TO FILL IN THE SELF-EMPLOYMENT TAX PAGES

If you want to explain any figures or clarify a point use the 'Additional information' boxes on your Self-employment form. Your notes may answer any questions the Tax Office may have and save them having to write to you or make an enquiry into your accounts.

Boxes 3.1 to 3.10: Business details

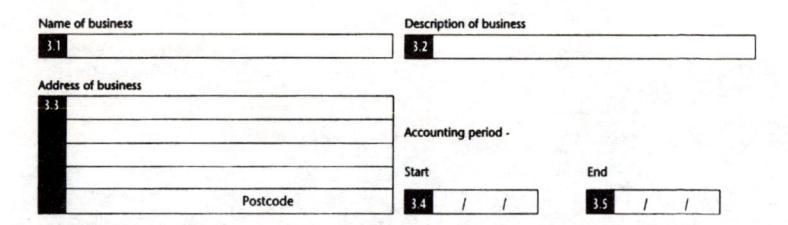

Name of business 3.1	Description of business 3.2
Address of business 3.3	Accounting period - Start 3.4 / / End 3.5 / /
Postcode	

Enter the name of your business – if do not have a business name enter your own name in box **3.1**, a brief description of your trade (for example builder) in box **3.2** and your trading address (or home address if you work from home) in box **3.3**. Fill in **Box 3.6** if any of these details have changed since your last Tax Return.

Note: If you have more than one business you **must** complete **Boxes**

SELF-EMPLOYMENT

3.1 to 3.3 on a separate set of Self-employment pages for each business.

Write the accounting period for which you are providing details of income and expenses in **Boxes 3.4** and **3.5**. Read the notes on page SEN2 of your Tax Return guide before filling in any of the remaining boxes. They will mainly apply to those who have changed accounting dates. And then fill in any dates such as the starting or closing date of your business or a change in accounting date.

BUSINESSES WITH A TURNOVER BELOW £15,000

Boxes 3.11 to 3.13: Income and expenses for businesses with a turnover below £15,000

Income and expenses - annual turnover below £15,000

If your annual turnover is £15,000 or more, **ignore** boxes 3.11 to 3.13.   Now fill in Page SE2

If your annual turnover is below £15,000, **fill in boxes 3.11 to 3.13 instead of Page SE2**. Read the Notes, page SEN2.

- Turnover, other business receipts and goods etc. taken for personal use   **3.11** £
- Expenses allowable for tax   **3.12** £

Net profit (put figure in brackets if a loss)   box 3.11 minus box 3.12 **3.13** £

If your annual turnover is more than this (remember if you have been trading for less than a year you must adjust your turnover proportionately) you must fill in page SE2.

If your *annual turnover* is less than £15,000 and you have more than one business you must complete a set of self-employment pages for each business.

Box 3.11: Turnover

Your turnover must include sales and other business receipts and:

☐ include the normal selling price of any goods you have taken for personal use or for your family or friends *less* any amount paid for them;

☐ include income which has been earned but not received. Note even if you have not issued a bill, you generally earn the income at the time the goods or services are provided;

FILLING IN YOUR TAX RETURN

- include expenses or debts you have incurred but not yet paid for;
- do not include enterprise allowance or business start-up allowance (that goes in **Box 3.88**);
- do not include interest received from your bank or building society (put that on your main Tax Return with other savings income).

Box 3.12: Expenses

Remember that you can only deduct *allowable* expenses and should not include *disallowable* expenses even if they are included in your accounts. A more detailed explanation of what you can and cannot claim is given in Part 2 of this book. Also see page SE5 of the Inland Revenue notes on Self-employment. An additional list is given on *Help Sheet IR221* (which you should request if you don't already have it).

Remember you cannot deduct:

- general provisions for bad debts – only specific debts written off;
- the cost of buying plant and machinery, cars or computers – these are capital assets and are included on page SE3 under 'Capital allowances'.

> **Tax tip:** If you make a payment that covers an expense for more than one accounting period (for instance 12 months of rent) only deduct the proportion that relates to the accounting period on your Tax Return.

Box 3.13: Profit/loss:

Your profit or loss is your income minus your expenses. If you made a loss write that figure in brackets.

The Tax Return advises you to go straight to page SE3. However, if you have drawn up your own accounts and are worried that you may have left something out, take a photocopy of page SE2 and work through **Boxes 3.14 to 3.52**.

> **Tax tip:** Read through the notes for page SE2 as you may find that you have forgotten to deduct an expense or have wrongly deducted something that is not allowed.

Now fill in page SE3 of your Tax Return.

SELF-EMPLOYMENT

BUSINESSES WITH A TURNOVER OF £15,000 OR MORE

Income and expenses - annual turnover £15,000 or more

You must fill in this Page if your annual turnover is £15,000 or more - read the Notes, page SEN2

If you were registered for VAT, do the figures in boxes 3.16 to 3.51, include VAT? **3.14** or exclude VAT? **3.15**

Sales/business income (turnover) **3.16** £

	Disallowable expenses included in boxes 3.33 to 3.50	Total expenses
• Cost of sales	**3.17** £	**3.33** £
• Construction industry subcontractor costs	**3.18** £	**3.34** £
• Other direct costs	**3.19** £	**3.35** £

Gross profit/(loss) **3.36** £
Other income/profits **3.37** £

A separate set of income and expenses pages (page SE2) must be filled in if you have more than one business or more than one set of accounts and your turnover is £15,000 or more a year.

Boxes 3.14 and 3.15: VAT:

If you are not registered for VAT you can claim any VAT back paid in your expenses boxes. Include VAT in the cost of each item. You don't have to tick **Box 3.14** or **3.15**.

Only tick **Boxes 3.14** or **3.15** if you are registered for VAT. You can either include VAT in **all** your figures including income and expenses, or you can exclude it in **all** cases.

If you include VAT write your net payment to Customs & Excise in *Box 3.50*. If you received a net repayment from Customs & Excise include this figure in **Box 3.37**. Read page SE4 of the Inland Revenue notes on Self-employment for more information.

Box 3.16: Turnover

Enter your sales/business income – remember turnover is all the money earned but not necessarily received (excluding enterprise allowance or Business Start up Allowance which go in **Box 3.87**) before you deduct business expenses.

Income from sales of goods or services are classed as being earned at the time of sale or when you provide them – so even if you do not receive payment for many months, your turnover should include the figures for goods and services provided in the

FILLING IN YOUR TAX RETURN

accounting year **not** just those that were paid for during the accounting year. Even if you have not issued a bill, you usually earn the income at the time the goods or services are provided. Make sure you do not include turnover from a previous accounting year by mistake.

Turnover also includes receipts in cash or in kind for goods sold or work done, commissions, etc. You should also include in your turnover any amounts you have paid for goods taken out of the business for your personal use or for your family and friends (the difference between this price and the normal selling price is included in **Box 3.54**).

Do not include any capital receipts – this is money you received or the part-exchange value on the sale of capital assets such as machinery or business equipment (this goes in **Boxes 3.61** to **3.70**). These assets are things you use in business rather than sell as part of your business.

Boxes 3.17 and 3.33: Cost of sales

These will be listed in your accounts. Cost of sales includes stock or raw materials or goods bought for resale.

Note that you must include items you have received but not yet paid for. Cost of sales can even include petrol if you are a taxi driver or run a haulage business as you are effectively buying fuel and selling it on. You can only normally claim for the costs of goods and raw materials used to make goods actually sold or to provide services. This is why stocktaking is so important. However, you can deduct the costs of raw materials that are part-way through manufacturing and costs incurred in large service contracts as *work-in-progress* costs. Ask for *Help Sheet 225* to help you work out the costs you can claim.

If you sell stock you must do your stocktaking at the end of the year and work out how much of your stock was actually sold. Take the value of stock and *work in progress on hand* at the start of the accounting year and add the value of any goods or raw materials bought during the accounting year. Then deduct stock and *work in progress on hand* at the end of the period. This is the amount you can deduct as *cost of sales* **not** the total value of all stock or raw materials purchased during the year.

SELF-EMPLOYMENT

> **Tax tip:** Under this method it is difficult to ascertain which stock was actually sold. You can either use the first in, first out method, charging the first purchase against sales until that is used up and leaving the second in stock, and then the second purchase against sales and so on. Or you can use the last in, first out method, deducting the last item bought against sales. Or you can average out purchases. As a result you can get varying figures for your cost of sales. It is up to a business to choose the method used but once chosen the business should stick with this method and it should give a fair approximation to what has actually happened.

Note: If your stock is to be sold for less than its cost (at a loss) you value the item at its **net realizable value** taking into account any losses and costs incurred before the stock is sold. This will reduce the value of your stock at the end of the accounting period and therefore increase your cost of sales.

If you run a service business and do not adjust your business profits to reflect work in progress at the start and end of the accounting year, you can leave the box blank.

Disallowable expenses in **Box 3.17** will include stock purchased but not for business purposes such as the fuel expenses of a taxi business which were for non-business use.

Boxes 3.18 and 3.34: Construction industry

There are special taxation rules for the construction industry. Businesses are required to deduct tax from subcontractors who are uncertificated. In this box include the gross amount – before deduction of tax if any tax was deducted.

Disallowable expenses will include payments made relating to non-business work.

Boxes 3.19 and 3.35: Other direct costs

This will include items that are not classed as 'cost of sales' (the cost of buying raw materials to make your goods or stock and other costs to provide your service) and not classed as 'business expenses' or costs of running your business. 'Direct' means the costs are an integral part of providing your goods or services – for instance leasing of milk quotas if you are a farmer – rather than hiring staff which is classed as a running cost. If you are in doubt ask your Tax Office for advice or make a note in the 'Additional information' box.

FILLING IN YOUR TAX RETURN

Box 3.36: Gross profit (loss)

Deduct your cost of sales and direct costs (and subcontractor costs if you are in the construction industry) from your turnover to give your gross profit or loss. **Losses must always be written in brackets not with a minus sign.** So if you made a loss of £4000 you would write (£4000) not -£4000.

Box 3.37: Other income

This includes income that does not come from sales of goods or services provided. Watch out for income that will be included elsewhere on your Tax Return. For instance, if you include bank and building society interest on your business account, this is not trading income. As such if you include the figure here make a note in **Box 3.58** so it can be deducted from your profits. Make sure you then include the same figure on page 3 of your main Tax Return under bank and building society interest.

Other income can be from rents – if you rent out part of your business premises and do not include this item on the Land and property form. Basically, include any other income that is not included in turnover (but not the sale of capital assets as these are included elsewhere).

Boxes 3.20 to 3.50: Business expenses

• Employee costs	3.20 £	3.38 £
• Premises costs	3.21 £	3.39 £
• Repairs	3.22 £	3.40 £
• General administrative expenses	3.23 £	3.41 £
• Motor expenses	3.24 £	3.42 £
• Travel and subsistence	3.25 £	3.43 £
• Advertising, promotion and entertainment	3.26 £	3.44 £
• Legal and professional costs	3.27 £	3.45 £
• Bad debts	3.28 £	3.46 £
• Interest	3.29 £	3.47 £
• Other finance charges	3.30 £	3.48 £
• Depreciation and loss/(profit) on sale	3.31 £	3.49 £
• Other expenses	3.32 £	3.50 £
	Put the total of boxes 3.17 to 3.32 in box 3.53 below	**Total expenses**

SELF-EMPLOYMENT

In the total expenses box write the total amount of business expenses **including** those that you are **not** allowed to offset against profits such as business entertaining. Then deduct the **disallowable** expenses and put them in the left-hand column. It is important for you to list disallowable expenses as you will have to add these to your profit before it is taxed. If you only record allowable expenses (which is unlikely) you do not have to fill in the disallowable column – but the Inland Revenue may want to ask you why.

A list of what you are and are not allowed to deduct is given on page SE5 of the Inland Revenue notes on Self-employment. An additional list is given on *Help Sheet IR221* (which you should request if you don't already have it). A list of some of the expenses that you may overlook – or try to claim when you are not allowed to – is given earlier in this book in Part 2. Read chapter 8 before filling in these boxes.

Apart from treading the fine line between what is allowable and disallowable, the only boxes you may find confusing are as follows.

Boxes 3.31 and 3.49: Depreciation and loss/(profit) on sale

These two boxes should both contain the depreciation in value of assets and losses incurred when these assets are sold. However, you are not allowed to deduct these as a business expense. As such the figures in both boxes should be the same – and will cancel each other out. If you sold assets at a profit deduct this profit from your losses and depreciation. Only include *fixed assets*. These will be listed on your *balance sheet* (the list of what your business owns and owes) if you have one. Fixed assets are items which are permanently necessary for your business such as machinery, cars, fixtures and fittings, your business premises or the lease on them. Do not include stock or cash. Working out whether or not you made a profit or loss when you sold one of these assets will be straightforward.

Calculating depreciation is a little more complicated. If you have a car you will be able to check how the value has depreciated (fallen) by looking in on the guides on sale in book shops and some newsagents. Other items, such as property, can be valued by a surveyor or by asking your local estate agent. Your Tax Office can also give you advice.

Remember, these figures cancel each other out because you cannot deduct depreciation or losses as a business expense.

Box 3.51: Total expenses

Add up your total expenses boxes (these should already include disallowable expenses so do not add them in again).

Box 3.52: net profit/(loss)

This is your gross profit/(loss) plus other income/profits minus expenses. Remember to write any loss in brackets.

TAX ADJUSTMENTS TO NET PROFIT OR LOSS

Boxes 3.53: Disallowable expenses

These are now added to your net profit as they are not tax deductible and as such have to be added to your taxable profits. Do not forget to include **Boxes 3.17** to **3.19** at the top of the column.

Box 3.54: Goods for personal use

Deduct the normal selling price of all goods taken out of your business for personal use (or for use by friends and family). If you included the price paid to your business for goods taken out for personal use in your turnover deduct this before writing in the normal selling price.

Box 3.55 and 3.57:

See capital allowances and balancing charges on page 102.

Box 3.56:

Simply add boxes **3.53**, and **3.54** and **3.55** together and unite in the total.

Box 3.58: Deductions from net profits

This covers an assortment of extras that are included elsewhere on your Tax Return (so they do not need to be taxed again under self-employment) and taxes you have already paid (you will not want to be taxed twice). This box reduces your tax liability by either reducing profits or increasing losses.

Deduct from profits (or add to losses) anything that is included in another part of your Tax Return (bank and building society interest), or anything that has already been taxed or is not liable to tax.

If you have income from abroad that has already been taxed and you want to claim tax credit relief you should write in the amount of foreign income you have received in **Box 3.58** and then include this income on the Foreign pages. Or you can simply claim back foreign tax you have already paid by putting the amount of tax deducted in this box.

If you do not think you should be paying tax on a particular receipt (income) or think you have already paid tax on items included in your turnover ask your Tax Office for advice on where to include these figures.

If you include a figure in this box you must explain why in the 'Additional information' box.

Box 3.59: Additions to net profit

Simply add figures in **Boxes 3.57** and **3.58** together.

Box 3.60: Net business profit (loss)

Follow the simple calculation instructions on your Tax Return to get your net profit (loss) for tax purposes.

CAPITAL ALLOWANCES AND BALANCING CHARGES

Read the tax-saving tips in Part 2, Chapter 8 of this book for information on how to calculate your capital allowances and balancing charges, what you can claim and what you cannot.

Boxes 3.61 to 3.70: Capital allowances

WARNING: If you are a new business and your accounting period is not 12 months you must either reduce or increase your allowances proportionately. So if you have only been in business for six months you can only claim half the capital allowance.

> **Tax tip:** A special tax break is given to small and medium-sized businesses (those with a turnover of £11.2 million) this year. **Any capital expenditure between 2 July 1997 and 1 July 1998 will qualify for a 50 per cent first-year allowance.** This means you can deduct 50 per cent of the costs in the first year, reducing to 25 per cent of the written-down value thereafter. From 2 July 1998 to 1 July 1999, the first year allowance will be 40 per cent. Note, that it does not matter when you incurred the expenditure during the tax year. Even if you buy an asset at the end of your accounting period you can deduct the entire 40 or 50 per cent. Only if your accounting period is less than 12 months will you have to reduce the allowance proportionately.

Follow the calculation instructions in Part 2, Chapter 8 of this book to work out your capital allowances or balancing charges.

The general *pool* of plant and machinery must be included in **Boxes 3.60** and **3.61**.

Other items must be calculated separately or in their own *pool*. Once you have completed the relevant boxes add up the total figures and write them in **Boxes 3.66** and **3.67**. Then follow the instructions for **Boxes 3.55** and **3.57** (see your tax return guide).

Boxes 3.71 to 3.88: Adjustments to arrive at taxable profit or loss

Use this section to adjust your profits by deducting overlap profits and offsetting your losses, or you can *carry forward* losses to offset against future profits or *carry back* to get a tax rebate on taxable profits in past years.

You can offset losses to reduce your tax liability in either the same year as you made the loss or in other accounting years. You can claim tax relief for your losses by making a deduction from:

☐ your income for the year (but include this in the Self-employment pages). This includes investment income and **earnings from employment**;
☐ as a deduction from your capital gains (include your figure in the Capital Gains pages);
☐ by reducing your business profits taxed in earlier years; or
☐ by carrying forward your losses to offset against future profits.

> **Tax tip:** If you are an employee and make a loss on your freelance earnings, you can offset these losses to reduce the tax you pay on your

> salary. However, you cannot set up a business purely to make a loss and reduce the tax you pay on other sources of income.

For information on how you can offset losses either against other income or past or future business income read Part 2 of this book.

Add in any other business income from enterprise allowance or business start-up allowance and any other amounts not included elsewhere in the Self-employment pages and include them in **Box 3.87**. A note in the Additional information' box on page 4 of the Self-employment pages will prevent the Tax Office asking about this. Then calculate your total taxable profits from this business.

Boxes 3.89 to 3.91: Class 4 National Insurance Contributions

These payments are collected by the Inland Revenue because they are based on the profits you make from your trade or profession. Note that you can no longer claim half your contributions against tax.

You do not have to pay Class 4 contributions for the 1997/98 year of assessment if:

- your profits are below the lower profits limit of £7010;
- you were a man aged over 65 or a woman aged over 60 at 6 April 1998;
- you were aged under 16 at 6 April 1998 (provided you have been granted an exception by the Contributions Agency);
- or you were not resident in the UK for tax purposes during 1997/98.

Read Part 1, Chapter 3 of this book for details on how much National Insurance you have to pay and the different types of National Insurance contributions you may have to make.

If you don't have to pay Class 4 National Insurance contributions or you have asked for a deferment tick **Box 3.89** and put a '0' in **Box 3.91**. Give an explanation as to why you do not need to pay National Insurance in the 'Additional information' box.

If you run more than one business you should also make sure that you do not pay more than the maximum. Ask for *Help Sheet IR220*.

You can offset losses from earlier years (if they have not already been used) to reduce profits chargeable to National Insurance by

FILLING IN YOUR TAX RETURN

entering the amount in **Box 3.90**. You can also deduct interest earned on savings or bank balances from your profits as you do not pay National Insurance on non-trading income.

Box 3.91: National Insurance Contributions due

If you don't want to calculate the amount of National Insurance you have to pay, the Tax Office will do this for you. Leave **Box 3.91** blank.
If you want to work out the figure:

1. Take the profit figure in **Box 3.60**.
2. Deduct any adjustments in **Box 3.90**.
3. This is your profit for National Insurance contributions.
4. Then deduct the exempt threshold of £7010.
5. You will then pay NICs on the first £17,170 of this figure.
6. Multiply this figure (up to a maximum of £17,170) by 6 per cent.
7. This is the amount of NICs due. (There is a maximum you can pay of £1030.)

Box 3.92

This relates to the construction industry only, and only to subcontractors who have had tax deducted at source. Enclose your SC605 with your tax return.

Boxes 3.94 to 3.110: Summary of Balance Sheet

You only need to fill this in if you have a balance sheet. This section is not used to calculate your tax bill.

'ADDITIONAL INFORMATION'

Explain any figures or accounting decisions here. This may answer questions that your Tax Office may want to ask you and prevent an inspector mounting an investigation into your accounts.

12

PARTNERSHIPS

You must fill in the Partnership pages of your Tax Return if, at any time during the 1997/98 tax year, you earned a share of profits, losses or income from a business which you carried out in partnership. This also covers income, profits and losses that you were entitled to – so even if you took no money out of the partnership you must still fill in the pages.

There are two types of Partnership pages to fill in.

☐ The short version is for those whose only partnership income was:
 – a share of trading or professional income;
 – interest with tax deducted from banks, building societies or deposit takers.
☐ The long or full version which covers all possible types of partnership income.

Which of these you fill in will not only depend on what type of income you receive but also on the *partnership statement* you receive.

You will need separate partnership pages for each partnership you are in and for each business the partnership carries on.

HOW TAX ON PARTNERSHIPS HAS CHANGED

Partners are now:

☐ taxed on the individual partner not the partnership;
☐ taxed on a current year basis.

From 31 January 1998 all partners have had to make their first tax payment as an individual partner paying their first instalment or *payment on account* for the 1997/98 tax year. There is no longer a tax assessment on the partnership. And you are now taxed on a current year basis which means you must include any profits for the accounting year ending in the April 1997 to April 1998 tax year on this Tax Return.

In the past some partnerships (those set up before 6 April 1994) were taxed on a preceding year basis which meant they were taxed on the accounting year ending in the previous tax year.

Note: When you join or leave a partnership, legally one partnership comes to an end and another begins even though the business carries on uninterrupted. To avoid this a partnership can elect for a *continuation*. This means that the business continues to be treated as though it had carried on as usual. Only if the business ceases to trade, does the partnership come to an end.

And from 1999, professionals in partnership will no longer benefit from cash accounting (they currently do not have to pay tax until they receive payment for work done instead of the accruals basis – accounting for work when done rather than when paid). The extra costs can spread over ten years.

PAPERWORK REQUIRED

You will need your Partnership returns and accounts, the Inland Revenue notes on Partnerships and any relevant *Help Sheets* listed at the beginning of the Inland Revenue notes. Filling in the forms is much easier than for the self-employed as you can rely on your Partnership accounts for much of the information.

TIPS FOR FILLING IN YOUR PARTNERSHIP TAX PAGES

Most of the information can be copied from your partnership accounts. Remember you are only taxed on your share of partnership profits (as determined by your partnership agreement). As with profits from self-employment you can offset losses against other income (such as income from employment) in the 1997/98 tax year or carry back losses to offset against profits from a previous year or carry them forward to offset against future profits.

See the notes in Self-employment for other tax tips as the same rules apply to partners and the self-employed.

13

SAVINGS INTEREST AND SHARE DIVIDENDS

Note: The following chapters look at the main eight pages of your Tax Return – the pages everyone has to fill in.

📄 PAPERWORK REQUIRED

It is essential that you have all the paperwork you need **before** filling in page 3 of the main tax return:

- [ ] bank and building society passbooks and any annual statements;
- [ ] unit trust and investment trust statements;
- [ ] National Savings documents;
- [ ] any other savings and investment literature you have;
- [ ] share dividend tax vouchers.

REMEMBER: You only need information about income received in the 6 April 1997 to 5 April 1998 tax year.

WHAT IF I DON'T HAVE ALL THE PAPERWORK?

- [ ] **Savings**: Ask your bank or building society to send you a tax deduction certificate. These annual statements are sent out automatically to those with larger savings. Or you can try to work out the interest you have earned, but it may be difficult calculating how much interest falls in the tax year.
- [ ] **Share dividends**: These should be paid to you with a tax voucher attached. If you have lost these ask the company share registrar for a duplicate.

FILLING IN YOUR TAX RETURN

☐ **Unit trusts and investment trusts**: You should ask the investment company for a duplicate of your annual statement.

Q10: SAVINGS AND INVESTMENTS

INCOME for the year ended 5 April 1998

Q10 Did you receive any income from UK savings and investments?   NO ☐   YES ☐   *If yes, fill in boxes 10.1 to 10.32 as appropriate. Include only your share from any joint savings and investments.*

Some savings accounts and share dividends are not taxable and as such do **not** have to be listed on your Tax Return. Note that even if tax **has** already been deducted you must still tick the *YES* box.

Although the question says did you 'receive any income' – this does not only mean that you actually received the money by taking income out of a savings or investment account or scheme. If your account was credited with interest or you earned income or interest that was then reinvested in your unit trust or other investment scheme, that **must** also be included.

Tax-free income from savings and investments

Do not tick the *YES* box if **all** your interest and dividend income is included in the following list:

☐ Personal Equity Plan (PEP) investments such as shares, unit trusts or investment trusts – however, if you have withdrawn more than £180 interest you will have to declare this. These will be replaced by the Individual Savings Account in April 1999;
☐ the first £70 of interest from a National Savings Ordinary Account;
☐ income from tax-free National Savings schemes:
    ○ Fixed Interest Savings Certificates;
    ○ Index-Linked Savings Certificates;
    ○ Children's Bonus Bonds;
    ○ any winnings from Premium Bonds;
☐ TESSAs (Tax Exempt Special Savings Accounts) providing you keep your money invested for at least five years. These will also be replaced by ISAs in 1999;
☐ SAYE (Save as You Earn) accounts – these were withdrawn from 1 December. 1994 although you can still invest in them to buy shares in the company you work for. If you still have a scheme, it

is tax free;
- [ ] dividends from ordinary shares in venture capital trusts.

Important note for those with joint accounts and joint investments

If you have a savings account or shares in a joint name only include **your** share of the income. This will usually be half. However, you can elect to split income differently but you must tell the Inland Revenue first. If you want to split income differently make a note in the Additional information box on page 8.

Important note for those who receive gross interest (without tax already deducted)

These are accounts that pay interest *gross*, which means **no** tax is deducted 'at source' by the bank or building society. Remember, just because interest is paid *gross* does not mean that it is not taxable.

Important note for those with more than one investment

If you have several building society accounts, unit trusts or share investments you must add up the total amount of each type of income before filling in each box. There is a blank form for you to use on page 28 of the Revenue Tax Return Guide.

If you stopped receiving interest from a particular source in the 1996/97 tax year, you may have paid too much tax. See page 9 of the Revenue tax return guide for more details.

HOW TO WORK OUT THE GROSS AMOUNT ON TAXED INTEREST AND DIVIDENDS

Gross simply means the amount before tax is deducted. To get this figure add together the *net* amount (the amount you received after tax) and the tax that was deducted. If you do not know how much tax has been deducted you will have to do a simple calculation. Tax is deducted at 20 per cent on savings interest and share dividends. But to find out how much tax has been deducted you must multiply the amount of interest by 25 per cent.

FILLING IN YOUR TAX RETURN

So if you earned £100 of gross interest:

20% tax × £100 = £20

£20 tax deducted from £100 gross interest = £80 net interest.

If you received £80 of net interest:

£80 × 25% (or divide by 4) = £20 tax deducted.

£80 net interest + £20 tax = £100 gross interest.

INTEREST

- Interest from UK banks, building societies and deposit takers
  - where no tax has been deducted — Taxable amount **10.1** £
  - where tax has been deducted — Amount after tax deducted **10.2** £ | Tax deducted **10.3** £ | Gross amount before tax **10.4** £

- Interest distributions from UK authorised unit trusts and open-ended investment companies (dividend distributions go below) — Amount after tax deducted **10.5** £ | Tax deducted **10.6** £ | Gross amount before tax **10.7** £

- National Savings (other than FIRST Option Bonds and the first £70 of interest from a National Savings Ordinary Account) — Taxable amount **10.8** £

- National Savings FIRST Option Bonds — Amount after tax deducted **10.9** £ | Tax deducted **10.10** £ | Gross amount before tax **10.11** £

- Other income from UK savings and investments (except dividends) — Amount after tax deducted **10.12** £ | Tax deducted **10.13** £ | Gross amount before tax **10.14** £

Box 10.1:

If you have any interest that is paid gross (without tax deducted), this should be totalled up and the amount written in **Box 10.1**.

Boxes 10.2 to 10.4:

See the notes on page 110 on how to calculate the gross amount before tax.

Boxes 10.5 to 10.7:

Only include unit trust interest payments, **not** dividends. If you received interest with no tax deducted simply enter '0' in **Box 10.6**. Remember, that even if you did not actually receive any interest but it was used to buy more units or shares, you must still show the

SAVINGS INTEREST AND SHARE DIVIDENDS

amount of interest you earned. Do not include any PEP investments unless you withdrew more than £180 interest from cash that had not yet been invested by your PEP manager. Do not include any 'equalization' payments as these are simply repayments of capital and therefore are not classed as income.

Box 10.8:

Do not include National Savings schemes that are not taxable such as Savings Certificates (see the list on page 109). And don't forget to deduct the first £70 of interest if you have an Ordinary Account. Include interest from the Ordinary Account, Investment Account, Deposit Bonds, Income Bonds and Pensioners' Guaranteed Income Bonds. Show the interest added to Capital Bonds during the year. Don't forget that tax is not deducted at source from these National Savings Schemes, so do not gross up your interest.

Boxes 10.9 to 10.11:

First Option Bonds are paid with tax already deducted. So you will need to gross up the amount and insert the amount of tax deducted.

Boxes 10.12 to 10.14:

Include any other interest you have earned that has not been entered into any of the other boxes. This will include interest from government stocks (gilts) including those bought through the National Savings Stock Register, interest on loans to individuals or organizations and interest from credit unions and friendly societies. If no tax has been deducted fill in the gross amount and do **not** work out how much tax should be deducted – or the Inland Revenue will assume you have already paid tax on this interest.

If you received income from an annuity (a lump-sum investment scheme that provides you with an income) and that annuity was **not** linked to a pension you will have to include that income in these boxes. Some of your income will be exempt as it is simply a repayment of your capital.

These boxes should also be used for those who have invested in discounted securities such as discounted bonds. See the Inland Revenue Guidance Notes and ask your financial adviser for further advice and information.

FILLING IN YOUR TAX RETURN

DIVIDENDS

	Dividend/distribution	Tax credit	Dividend/distribution plus credit
• Dividends and other qualifying distributions from UK companies	10.15 £ 224	10.16 £ 56	10.17 £ 280
• Dividend distributions from UK authorised unit trusts and open-ended investment companies	10.18 £	10.19 £	10.20 £

	Dividend	Notional tax	Dividend plus notional tax
• Scrip dividends from UK companies	10.21 £	10.22 £	10.23 £
• Foreign income dividends from UK companies	10.24 £	10.25 £	10.26 £
• Foreign income dividend distributions from UK authorised unit trusts and open-ended investment companies	10.27 £	10.28 £	10.29 £

		Notional tax	Taxable amount
• Non-qualifying distributions and loans written off	10.30 £	10.31 £	10.32 £

Boxes 10.15 to 10.17:

Simply copy the information from your share dividend vouchers. Dividends are the income you receive on shares. Do not include foreign income dividends or scrip dividends (where you receive extra shares instead of a cash dividend). Note that investment trusts are UK stock market quoted companies so you should put your dividend details in these boxes, unless you invested via a PEP.

Boxes 10.18 to 10.20:

This box is for dividends from unit trusts and a newer type of collective investment scheme known as OEICs (open-ended investment companies) which are similar to unit trusts. Remember, that even if your dividends were used to buy more units or shares you are still treated as though you earned these dividends and must declare them. Your money will be reinvested in this way if you have purchased 'accumulation' units. Do not include any 'equalization' payments as these are repayments of capital and are therefore not classed as income.

SAVINGS INTEREST AND SHARE DIVIDENDS

Boxes 10.21 to 10.23:

If you take shares instead of a cash dividend this is known as a scrip dividend. These are taxed in the same way as other dividends and you are taxed on 'the appropriate amount in cash'. This is paid after tax so write the amount in **Box 10.21** and work out the notional tax (by dividing by 4 or multiplying by 25 per cent.) Add these figures together and write the total in **Box 10.23**.

Boxes 10.24 to 10.29:

The same rules apply as for UK dividends and unit trusts. If the dividends are foreign your dividend voucher will show the amounts.

Boxes 10.30 to 10.32:

Non-qualifying distributions include bonus or redeemable shares and loans written off by companies. See your Tax Return Guide for more information.

HOW TO USE THE INFORMATION IN QUESTION 10 TO SAVE TAX:

Now that you have filled in the answers to **Q10** you can look at ways to reorganize your finances to save tax. Unfortunately you cannot make tax savings for the 1997/98 tax year as that has already ended. But you can save tax for future years.

> **Tax tips:**
>
> ☐ If you are married and one partner is a higher-rate taxpayer while the other is a non-taxpayer or pays tax at the lower or basic rate, you will save tax by putting all or most of the investment into the name of the partner who pays the least tax. You cannot backdate the way you split income so you will not save tax on your April 1998 Tax Return as the change only takes place from the date you make a declaration. Ask your Tax Office for advice and for Form 17. If you put all of your investments into the name of the partner who pays the least tax this must be an outright 'gift'. Otherwise the Inland Revenue may believe that you have not actually transferred the investment. By splitting your investments you

FILLING IN YOUR TAX RETURN

can also save on Capital Gains Tax – particularly if one partner does not use up all of their Capital Gains Tax allowance or pays the tax at a lower rate.

☐ Some £767 million of tax is wasted by unit trust, investment trust and share investors who do not make the most of PEPs – personal equity plans. You can invest up to £6000 in a main PEP and £3000 in a single-share PEP this year. No Income Tax is payable on dividends or other income and you can sell your investment free of Capital Gains Tax. Although these will be withdrawn in April 1999 and replaced by the Individual Savings Account all savings will still be free of Income and Capital Gains Tax.

☐ Consider tax-free savings schemes. Currently only TESSAs – the Tax-Exempt Special Savings Acount – and some National Savings schemes are available. TESSAs must be held for a minimum of five years and will be replaced in April 1999 by the new Individual Savings Account although existing TESSAs can continue for a further five years. You will be able to transfer your TESSA capital into the ISA.

☐ Income from savings and share dividends are taxed at 20 per cent with this tax deducted from your interest or dividends before they are paid to you. But basic-rate taxpayers who pay tax at 23 per cent do **not** have to pay an extra 3 per cent so make a tax saving. However, higher-rate taxpayers must pay the full 40 per cent tax so must pay an extra 20 per cent tax on top of that already deducted. Remember, your savings income is **added** to all your other income when working out your tax. This means that interest and dividends can push you into the higher-rate tax bracket.

☐ If you do not need your investment income, consider switching your investments into schemes that give you capital growth rather than income. This is because most or all of the investment will be taxed under Capital Gains Tax, which taxes the profits you make when you sell an investment instead of the income you earn from that investment. The allowance for Capital Gains is higher than that for Income Tax – £6500 for the 1997/98 tax year. Many taxpayers fail to use up this allowance and provided your total profits from sales of investments and other assets is less than £6500 you will pay no tax.

☐ Offshore investments earn interest gross (without tax deducted). Although you must declare this income, you do not have to pay tax on it until nine months after the end of the tax year. You can therefore reinvest your interest and earn interest on this interest to boost your return. The same applies to dividends.

☐ If you want to boost your savings rate consider a local authority bond, also known as a yearly bond. Investments start at £1000. However, if you

SAVINGS INTEREST AND SHARE DIVIDENDS

sell your investment before the six-monthly interest payment is made, you should make a capital gain rather than earning interest and therefore will escape any Income Tax. However, this only applies if the nominal value of these does not exceed £5000. The same rules apply to gilts if you convert interest into capital if sold 'cum interest'.

Tax warning

If you put savings into your children's name or into a children's account and the child is under 18 you – as the parent – may have to pay tax. If the interest is above £100 gross a year you will pay tax on the whole income (not just the proportion above £100). The same applies if you set up a *trust* fund to pay income to your children. To get round this rule, a grandparent or aunt and uncle can set up a savings or investment scheme for your child and the child will not pay tax unless income exceeds the personal allowance of £4195 (for the 1998/99 tax year).

14

PENSIONS, SOCIAL SECURITY BENEFITS, MAINTENANCE PAYMENTS AND OTHER INCOME

📄 PAPERWORK REQUIRED

This will include:

- ☐ details of any state benefits or pensions you received;
- ☐ your P60 if you receive a company pension;
- ☐ details of any income taken from a personal pension plan;
- ☐ records of how much you received from any annuities purchased to give you an income for life.

Q11: STATE PENSIONS AND BENEFITS

■ *State pensions and benefits*

	Taxable amount for 1997-98
• State Retirement Pension	11.1 £
• Widow's Pension	11.2 £
• Widowed Mother's Allowance	11.3 £
• Industrial Death Benefit Pension	11.4 £
• Jobseeker's Allowance	11.5 £
• Invalid Care Allowance	11.6 £
• Statutory Sick Pay and Statutory Maternity Pay paid by the Department of Social Security	11.7 £

	Tax deducted	Gross amount before tax
• Taxable Incapacity Benefit	11.8 £	11.9 £

PENSIONS, BENEFITS, MAINTENANCE, OTHER INCOME

Many state benefits are **not** taxable and as such do **not** need to be included on your Tax Return.

Taxable state benefits include:

- ☐ state retirement pension and widow's pension;
- ☐ widowed mother's allowance;
- ☐ industrial death benefit pension;
- ☐ jobseeker's allowance;
- ☐ invalid care allowance;
- ☐ statutory sick pay and statutory maternity pay (only include in this section if paid by the Department of Social Security. If paid by your employer it will be included in your total pay for the year and tax will have been deducted by your employer
- ☐ taxable incapacity benefit.

Tick the **YES** box if you received any of the above benefits **and/or** if you received **any** other pension.

Boxes 11.1 to 11.9:

This section is very straightforward. There are only two things you must take care over.

1. You must enter the full amount you were *entitled to* in the tax year from 6 April 1997 to 5 April 1998. So if you receive a payment quarterly or monthly do not add up the equivalent amount over a year. The figure you give must be for the tax year only. So if you receive a payment on 10 April and some of this included benefits or pensions before 6 April, you must exclude the amount payable for the pre-6 April period.
2. You must ensure you do not include any non-taxable benefits.

If you are not sure what figures to include or want to check the figures you can ask the Benefit Office (part of the Department of Social Security) for a statement of taxable state benefits you have received.

If you received a combined payment from the Benefit Office ask for this to be broken down into component parts. For instance, if your Income Support includes your pension and attendance allowance ask for this to be split into separate amounts so that your attendance allowance is not taxed.

FILLING IN YOUR TAX RETURN

A full list of what should be included in this section is given on page 13 of your Inland Revenue guidance notes.

Box 11.1:

State pensions include:

- ☐ basic pension;
- ☐ state earnings related pension (SERPS);
- ☐ graduated pension;
- ☐ age addition if you are over 80;
- ☐ incapacity addition or addition for dependent adult;
- ☐ any increases paid by the DSS to uprate a guaranteed minimum pension.

Do not include the Christmas bonus or any increase in pension for a dependent child.

If you receive a war widow's pension or are a dependant of a deceased former member of the Forces or Merchant Navy, ask for *Help Sheet IR310* from the Orderline on 0645 000 404. This will tell you if you can receive your pension tax free and, if not, how much tax you need to pay.

Remember, pensions received from another country must be included on the Foreign pages.

Boxes 11.2 to 11.7:

Simply enter the total amount you were entitled to in the tax year.

Boxes 11.8 to 11.9:

The reason why you are asked to include the tax deducted is that some incapacity benefits are taxable. However payments, in the first 28 weeks of capacity are **not** taxable. Ask the Department of Social Security for details and figures.

PENSIONS, BENEFITS, MAINTENANCE, OTHER INCOME

Q11: OTHER PENSIONS AND RETIREMENT ANNUITIES

- Pensions (other than State pensions) and retirement annuities

Amount after tax deducted	Tax deducted	Gross amount before tax
11.10 £	11.11 £	11.12 £

- Deduction
  - see the note for box 11.3 on page 14 of your Tax Return Guide

Amount of deduction
11.13 £

These include:

- ☐ pensions from your former employer or your late spouse's former employer's company pension scheme;
- ☐ personal pension plans – including income withdrawals where no annuity has been purchased;
- ☐ income from any additional pension from free-standing additional voluntary contributions (FSAVCs). But refunds of surplus AVCs should go in **Boxes 12.10** to **12.12**. These will be refunds because you have paid in more than is allowed as a percentage of your income;
- ☐ income from retirement annuity contracts (an annuity is purchased from your personal pension fund on retirement to provide you with an income for life).

Purchased life annuities (lump-sum investments that give you an income for the rest of your life) which are **not** linked to a pension should also be included in **Boxes 11.10** to **11.12**.

Boxes 11.10 to 11.12:

If you receive a pension from an occupational pension scheme (from a former employer's scheme) this will be paid to you with tax already deducted in the same way as salaries are paid after PAYE. You should be sent a form P60 by 31 May 1998 showing you how much was paid in the tax year and how much tax was deducted.

Income from a personal pension plan (when you retire your fund is used to buy an annuity to give you an income) should also be included. If you have not yet purchased an annuity, any income taken out of your pension fund should be included. Ask your plan provider for details of income received. As with employer pensions, annuity income is taxed at source under PAYE (for personal

FILLING IN YOUR TAX RETURN

pensions) and with basic rate tax deducted (from retirement annuity contracts).

Total up all the pensions before filling in the boxes. Do **not** include any lump sums you received on retirement as these are usually tax free.

Box 11.13:

You will only need to fill in this box if:

- ☐ you worked for an overseas government or are a dependant or widow of someone who did;
- ☐ your pension was increased because you retired on the grounds of disability by work injury or because of a work-related illness;
- ☐ your pension is paid for war injuries or other disability as a result of military service.

See page 14 of your Tax Return Guide for further information.

Tax tips:

- ☐ If you are coming up to retirement and do not need to take your pension you can defer it and take it at a later date. Not only will this boost your income later on (when you might need the extra money) but you can defer paying tax on the pension until you receive it. So if you have a high income now and will have a much lower income later on, you will be taxed on your state pension or company pension at a lower rate.
- ☐ When you retire you can take a tax-free lump sum from your pension. This can be a maximum of 25 per cent of the fund if you have a personal pension or one-third of your final pay if you are in a final-salary company pension scheme. You may be better off investing this cash in a tax-free savings scheme than purchasing an annuity which is taxable or using the lump sum to reduce any loans or mortgages.

Q12: MAINTENANCE RECEIVED AND GAINS ON LIFE INSURANCE POLICIES

This section covers a wide range of extras.

PENSIONS, BENEFITS, MAINTENANCE, OTHER INCOME

📄 PAPERWORK REQUIRED

This will include:

- [ ] details of any maintenance or alimony payments you received and documents detailing the court orders, Child Support Agency or other agreements made;
- [ ] details of any taxable UK life insurance policies (your life insurance company or friendly society should have sent you a chargeable event certificate);
- [ ] details of any refunds of surplus additional voluntary contributions (the top-up pension schemes linked to your company pension scheme).

	Income receivable	Exempt amount	Income less exempt amount
• Taxable maintenance or alimony	12.1 £ 3000	12.2 £ 1830	12.3 £ 1170

Boxes 12.1 to 12.3: Taxable maintenance or alimony

Not all maintenance income **received** from a former spouse or your parents is taxable. If you receive *voluntary* maintenance payments or payments under an agreement or *court order* made **on or after 15 March 1988** you are covered by the 'new rules' and do **not** have to pay any tax on what you receive and you do not have to include these payments on your Tax Return.

Different or 'old rules' apply to maintenance payments agreed or made by court order **before 15 March 1988**. These maintenance payments are taxable but you won't have to pay tax on all the maintenance payments you receive.

Boxes 12.1 to 12.3:

Only fill these boxes in if you come under the 'old rules' ie your maintenance payments were agreed before 15 March 1988. Agreed maintenance payments include those:

- [ ] made under a court order (the 15 March 1988 deadline is extended to 30 June 1988 if the application to the court was made

before 15 March 1988);
- written and verbal agreements (provided the Inland Revenue received details of these by 30 June 1988);
- court orders, CSA assessments and written agreements made after 15 March 1988 but only varying or adding to any pre-15 March 1988 payments.

Do **not** fill in this box if:

- the payments are voluntary (regardless of when they were first paid);
- you are over 21 and receive maintenance payments from your parents;
- the person making the payments has written to you stating they have made an election for the 'new rules' to apply.

If your maintenance payments have increased, only write in the amount you were due to receive in the 6 April 1988 to 5 April 1989 tax year in **Box 12.1**. You do not have to pay tax on any maintenance payments above this amount.

If you receive less now than you did in the 1988/89 tax year, you will pay tax on the lower amount. So write the amount you received in the 1997/98 tax year in **Box 12.1**.

In some cases *the first £1830 of maintenance payments is free of tax*. Anything over this sum is taxable. You will qualify for the tax allowance if:

- the payments are from your separated or former spouse;
- they are for yourself or for the support of a child aged under 21;
- you have **not** remarried;
- during the 1997/98 tax year you did not live with the separated or former spouse who pays the maintenance.

Note: The payments can only be paid to the spouse. Payments to children or stepchildren are taxable on the full amount.

The exempt amount in **Box 12.2** will either be the £1830 tax-free allowance or the amount you received if this is lower. The amount over this sum should be written in **Box 12.3** and the total amount received in **Box 12.1**.

PENSIONS, BENEFITS, MAINTENANCE, OTHER INCOME

> **Tax tips:**
>
> ☐ If your maintenance payments have been increased since 6 April 1989 you do not have to pay tax on the extra amounts.
> ☐ Try to get your former spouse to elect that the payments be treated under the 'new rules' as qualifying maintenance payments. Under the 'new rules' you will not pay any tax. However, your separated or former spouse may lose out. The payer can claim an Income Tax reduction on the amount he or she pays up to a maximum of the married couple's allowance (£1830). But he or she will only receive tax relief at 15 per cent (£275) and will no longer be able to claim tax relief at his or her higher rate on payments above this level. But if you receive maintenance you will gain.

If you want more information ask for leaflet *IR93: Separation, divorce and maintenance payments* by ringing the Orderline on 0645 000 404.

Boxes 12.4 to 12.9: Gains on UK Life Insurance policies

- Gains on UK life insurance policies (without notional tax) — Number of years **12.4** — Amount of gain **12.5** £

- Gains on UK life insurance policies (with notional tax) — Number of years **12.6** — Notional tax **12.7** £ — Amount of gain **12.8** £

Do not think you have to fill this in just because your life insurance policy has matured (paid out). Most life insurance policies are **not** taxable.

To be exempt from tax you must have a *qualifying policy*. This simply means that it qualifies as being tax exempt. These are policies which require you to pay premiums monthly or annually for at least ten years. However, don't think the returns are completely tax free. The insurance company has to pay tax on its profits (unless it is a friendly society). Your policy is treated as though you have paid basic-rate tax. This is known as *notional* tax. Even if you are a non-taxpayer you cannot reclaim this tax.

Non-qualifying policies are generally single-premium policies – where you make a one-off investment. They are not bought as life insurance policies but as investments and are often called investment bonds.

You will pay tax on the difference between what is paid out (the maturity proceeds) and the amount you paid in (the premiums paid). Some of these policies allow you to make 5 per cent withdrawals every year. The life assurance company will give you a 'chargeable event' certificate showing that a potentially taxable withdrawal has been made.

However, some *qualifying* policies may also be taxable. If you cash in a policy before ten years are up, provided you have been paying regular premiums for at least three-quarters of the term of the policy or ten years (which ever is the lower), your gain remains tax free. If you cash in the policy before then, your policy is treated as a *non-qualifying policy* and you will be taxed. This is why you have to write the number of years you have held the policy on your Tax Return.

If you are in doubt as to whether your policy is taxable or not ask your insurance company.

You may also be taxed on a non-qualifying policy if you:

☐ make a partial withdrawal from your policy;
☐ payments are made on death;
☐ you take out a loan against your policy from the insurance company; or
☐ you sell your policy.

Only add up gains from policies if you bought a cluster of identical policies with identical gains. Otherwise you must include details of **all** policies in the 'Additional information' box on page 8 of your Tax Return and then add up the total gains and put them in **Boxes 12.5, 12.7** and **12.8**. Do not fill in **Boxes 12.4** or **12.6**.
Note: Do not include any gains from foreign policies. These go on the Foreign pages.

Boxes 12.4 and 12.5:

These boxes are for friendly society policies and certain life annuities that are not treated as having being taxed at the basic rate. Write the number of **complete years** – not part years – that you have held your policy for in the first box. If, in the past, you have made part-withdrawals, part-sale or taken out a loan against the policy write the number of complete years since then. To work out your gain deduct the premiums from the amount you received.

Boxes 12.6 to 12.8:

This is for gains from life insurance policies bought from companies

PENSIONS, BENEFITS, MAINTENANCE, OTHER INCOME

that pay tax on their life insurance funds. As explained above *notional* tax at 23 per cent is deducted. Again write in the number of complete years – or complete years since the last part withdrawal, loan or part-sale.

For more information ask for **Help Sheet IR320: Gains on UK life insurance policies.**

> **Tax tips:**
>
> ☐ Basic-rate taxpayers do not have to pay any additional tax on taxable gains from life insurance polices, life annuities and capital redemption policies. You only have to pay tax at 40 per cent if you are a higher-rate taxpayer. This is because life insurance policies are treated as though they have already been taxed at the basic rate. So, if you are considering making a part or full withdrawal, select a year when you are a basic-rate taxpayer.
>
> ☐ If you have a non-qualifying investment bond you can usually take out 5 per cent of the fund each year without paying tax at the time. But at the end of the policy, the amount you have withdrawn will be added to the gain to work out the tax due. So if you are then a lower-rate taxpayer (for instance you have retired) there will be no extra tax to pay. If you do not withdraw the full 5 per cent each year, you can carry this amount forward (use this allowance in future years).
>
> ☐ The proceeds of a taxable life insurance policy or investment bond may push you into the 40 per cent tax bracket. This is because the income you receive is added to your total income and only then is your top rate of tax calculated. If you only pay higher-rate tax because of the life insurance gain, you can reduce the amount of tax you pay using *top-slicing relief*. This means that you work out your average yearly gain over the number of years that the policy ran. You add this average yearly gain to your 1997/98 income. If you no longer fall into the higher-rate tax bracket once this is added to your other income, you will not have to pay higher-rate tax. Or you may find that you only have a small amount of income in the higher-rate tax bracket, so you only have to pay 40 per cent tax on part of your gain.

The reason why you get this tax concession is that the gains in **Boxes 12.5** and **12.8** do not take into account the fact that gains may have accrued over a number of years. However, you cannot use top-slicing relief to increase your age-related allowances by reducing your total income.

You will need a separate Tax Calculation Guide SA154 for this and should **not** use the standard calculation guide SA151.

HOW TO CALCULATE NOTIONAL TAX:

Most life companies will have already paid tax on their profits, capital gains and income from investments. This is the 'notional' tax that you have effectively paid on your life insurance policy. To work it out simply deduct 23 per cent of the amount you receive (the figure in **Box 12.8**) and write this in the notional tax box. Friendly societies do not have to pay notional tax so include the gain in **Box 12.5**. If you are unsure whether notional tax has been deducted or not ask your investment adviser or the life insurance/investment company. You may have been sent a chargeable event certificate showing gains you have made and tax paid.

Box 12.9:

This will only apply if you have made taxable withdrawals during the term of the policy and they have already been taxed. You must include the amount so that the amount taxed as investment income is not more than the total gain.

- Refunds of surplus additional voluntary contributions

Amount received	Notional tax	Amount plus notional tax
12.10 £	12.11 £	12.12 £

Boxes 12.10 to 12.12: SURPLUS ADDITIONAL VOLUNTARY CONTRIBUTIONS

When you pay into a company pension scheme you receive tax relief at your top rate of tax. That is 40p for every £1 you invest if you are a higher-rate taxpayer. However, this tax break is restricted. You can only pay in 15 per cent of your earnings if you are in a company scheme and your pension on retirement cannot exceed two-thirds of final salary subject to an earnings cap of £84,000 for the 1997/98 tax year. So that gives a maximum pension of £56,000 a year.

Enter the total amount of the surplus AVC (not the amount of refund you received) in **Box 12.12**, the amount of refund you actually received after tax in **Box 12.10** and the tax deducted in **Box 12.11**.

The surplus additional voluntary contributions box will not apply to those who invest in free-standing AVCs as in this case the personal pension plan provider is obliged to repay the contributions in full and you will not get tax relief.

PENSIONS, BENEFITS, MAINTENANCE, OTHER INCOME

Q13: OTHER INCOME

📋 PAPERWORK REQUIRED

This will include:

- ☐ details of any income not included anywhere else on your tax return;
- ☐ records of any isolated casual, freelance or artistic income;
- ☐ details of any patent rights you have sold for a capital lump sum;
- ☐ annual payments from UK unauthorized unit trusts;
- ☐ annual payments paid by former employers which are not pension payments.

This is a chance for you to include anything you have not been able to include elsewhere. In some cases this may be because you did not know where to include this income and in other cases it will be because you want to use the losses to reduce (offset) the profits of another type of income.

WARNING: Only fill in this section after you have completed the supplementary pages for income from employment self-employment, share schemes, etc. If you don't, you could find that the information should have been included elsewhere on your Tax Return.

	Amount after tax deducted	Tax deducted	Amount before tax
• Other income	13.1 £	13.2 £	13.3 £

Boxes 13.1 to 13.3

Although casual work is normally classed as employment, if you received a one-off payment for freelance or consultancy work or a commission it may not be classed as income from employment. If that is the case, you can include it here. Profits from isolated literary or artistic activities could be included under self-employment, but if they are not, include them here. If your income counts as a 'trade' you will have to include the figures on the Self-Employment, Land and property or Partnership pages.

FILLING IN YOUR TAX RETURN

Read the list on page 16 of your Inland Revenue notes to check for any items you may have missed and look through your bank statements to see if you have forgotten to include any other items of income. Remember, if you fail to declare some income and the Inland Revenue finds out (either from an employer or even from an informer) you could face penalties.

The following should be included in 'other income':

- *Permanent health insurance* is an insurance that pays out should you be too ill to work. You **only** have to include payments from insurance policies taken out by a **former** employer and if you contributed to the premiums a proportion (equal to the proportion you paid) will be exempt. If you took out your own policy this is **not** taxable. If you received sickness or disability payments from an employer these must be included in the Employment pages.
- *Cashbacks* or *incentive payments* should also be taxed although few realize this. If you receive cash, a car, holiday or had a personal liability waived (for instance a loan written off) as an incentive to buy something (such as a car) or take out a mortgage, you may be taxed on it. Generally, if the cashback is a one-off payment it should escape Income Tax. If you are worried ask the company or person who gave you the incentive.
- Income you received from a business you are no longer involved in (although you can opt to have this taxed as income of the year in which the business ceased by using **Box 22.5**) is known as *post cessation income*. It can include recovered bad debts and royalties. Again you can deduct expenses before filling in **Box 13.3**. See page 17 of your Tax Return Guide for more information. If the income is purely from a change in the way the profits of a business are calculated you should ask your Tax Office which expenses you can deduct before filling in **Box 13.3**.
- Accrued income securities such as *interest-bearing securities* including those you can buy to invest in building societies at an above average fixed rate of interest (these are known as *permanent interest-bearing shares or PIBS*). Also include government loan stock (but not gilts) and company loan stock. No tax is payable if the nominal value of all accrued income securities held in the tax year did not exceed £5000. However, you should still fill in the box. Shares and other interest received have already been dealt with in *Q10*. Only include those which had an interest payment between 6 April 1997 and 5 April 1998.

PENSIONS, BENEFITS, MAINTENANCE, OTHER INCOME

This applies even when you sold these securities but the next interest due fell in this period. See page 17 of your Inland Revenue guidance notes for more information and *Help Sheet IR325*.

If you have more than one type of 'other income' you must add up the total amount. An explanation on the 'Additional information' page may save the Tax Office having to contact you. Ask for *Help Sheet IR325: Other income* which has a copy of a working sheet.

Only fill in **Box 13.2** if tax was deducted from your income.

> **Tax tip**
>
> Do not forget to deduct capital allowances and expenses incurred in earning any income. The Self-employment pages detail the types of expenses you can deduct and how to claim capital allowances if you bought any items of equipment to help you earn the extra income. You only have to include the amount you make as a profit in **Box 13.3** – so deduct any expenses before filling in this box. Expenses must be spent solely to earn the income and cannot be spent on things you intend to keep for a while – these need to be deducted as a capital allowance. Ask your Tax Office or tax adviser if you can deduct capital allowances. Expenses cannot be deducted from annual payments.

Write the total amount of other income you received – or were entitled to receive whether or not it was paid to you – in **Box 13.3**. If after deducting any expenses you made a loss, enter '0' in **Box 13.3** and fill in the loss in **Box 13.60**.

Total up any tax that was deducted in **Box 13.2**, and the amount paid to you after tax was deducted in **Box 13.1**. If no tax was deducted leave the tax box blank. Help Sheet IR325 has a working sheet you can use to add up the figures if you have more than one type of 'other income'.

> **Tax tip**
>
> If you invest in PIBS, corporate bonds or government loan stock the rate of return can be high and you can avoid tax by ensuring that the total value of all accrued interest income securities held at any time is £5000 or less.

You can use *losses* (where the amount you have earned does not cover your expenses) to reduce the tax on the same type of income in either this year or future years. In some cases losses can be used

FILLING IN YOUR TAX RETURN

to reduce the tax on other types of income. If you have filled in the Self-employment pages you will already know that you can use losses made in your business to reduce the amount of tax you pay on your employment or savings income. The same applies to items you list under 'other income'. For instance, you can offset debts from a business you no longer run against one-off freelance earnings.

But not all types of losses can be offset against other income. See IR325 for a working sheet of what can and cannot be offset.

If you do not use up your losses this year you can use them to reduce your tax in future years. This is known as *carrying forward*. Then the next year you bring them forward.

Losses included in the other income section can be used to reduce the tax on:

☐ casual earnings;
☐ one-off freelance income (but not regular work);
☐ rare literary earnings (articles or poems being published);
☐ isolated artistic earnings;
☐ sale of patent rights;
☐ and a few less common types of earnings.

If you include other income and want to use losses to reduce the tax on this ask for form *IR325*.

If you made losses in past years and did not have enough profits to offset these against (and you specified that you wanted to carry or bring forward these losses) write the figure in **Box 13.4**.

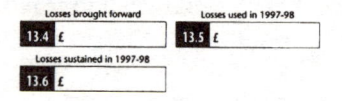

Losses brought forward	Losses used in 1997-98
13.4 £	13.5 £

Losses sustained in 1997-98
13.6 £

Write in **Box 13.5** the amount of these previous years' losses you are offsetting in 1997/98. If your losses are less than your 1997/98 profits in **Box 13.3** you must use up the whole amount. However, you can only do this if you are allowed to offset these losses against the type of income included in **Box 13.3**. So if your previous losses were for isolated artistic earnings you will not be able to offset these against permanent health insurance payments included in this section of your tax return.

Note: You cannot set losses against annual payments from unit trusts or from former employers.

PENSIONS, BENEFITS, MAINTENANCE, OTHER INCOME

In **Box 13.6** enter the total amount of your losses. Losses you cannot use this year and you want to carry forward to offset against future profits from similar income should be recorded on IR325.

Do not include losses from a discontinued business, called *post cessation losses*. These go in **Box 15.11**.

15

TAX RELIEF ON PENSIONS, MORTGAGES, CHARITABLE GIVING AND OTHER LOANS AND INVESTMENTS

Tax relief reduces your tax bill by giving you tax back or reducing the amount of tax you have to pay. In most cases you get tax relief at the top rate of tax you pay although some reliefs such as MIRAS (mortgage interest tax relief) are *restricted* to 15 per cent.

Some tax relief is given *at source* which means you do not have to claim it and get it automatically even if you are a non-taxpayer.

However, in other cases even when tax relief is given at source – for instance on personal pension contributions – if you want to claim higher-rate tax relief you may have to ask for it.

You can only claim higher-rate tax relief if you pay higher-rate (40 per cent) tax and you can only claim tax relief at 40 per cent on income that is taxed at 40 per cent.

This chapter deals with tax relief for:

- pension contributions including additional voluntary contributions;
- vocational training payments;
- interest on qualifying loans including mortgages;
- maintenance payments;
- investments in venture capital trusts or enterprise investment schemes;
- payments to charities;
- payments to trade unions or friendly societies for death benefits;

TAX RELIEF

- costs incurred after the close of a business (post cessation expenses);
- losses on relevant discounted securities.

Note: Mortgages that are part of MIRAS (mortgage interest relief at source) do not have to be included on your Tax Return as mortgage relief is given automatically.

Q14: PENSION CONTRIBUTIONS

📄 PAPERWORK REQUIRED

This will include:

- details of any contributions to personal pension plans or retirement annuity contracts if you are self-employed, in partnership or an employee.

This section covers:

- personal pensions taken out by employees who are not in company pension schemes;
- personal pension schemes (and old style personal pensions known as *retirement annuity contracts*) taken out by the self-employed.

If you have one of these pensions tick the *YES* box.

You get tax relief at your highest rate on contributions to personal pension plans. So for every £1 you invest you get 40p in tax relief if you are a higher-rate taxpayer.

There are limits on the contributions you can pay for each year. You cannot pay more than a set percentage of your *net relevant earnings*. This will be your pay plus bonuses if you are employed minus any expenses or payroll donations to charity. If you are **self-employed** or in **partnership** the net relevant earnings are your taxable business profits (your turnover minus your expenses figure in **Box 3.88**) or your share of the partnership profits (**Box 4.19**), or if you have profits from furnished holiday lettings the profit in **Box 5.14**.

FILLING IN YOUR TAX RETURN

With personal pensions you can only pay contributions on net relevant earnings up to the £84,000 *earnings cap* in the 1997/98 tax year. This earnings cap increases at the start of a new tax year, for 1998/99 it is £87,600. However, there is no earnings cap on retirement annuities.

Tables 15.1 and 15.2 give the maximum contributions you can make to a personal pension or retirement annuity plan. The amount you can contribute rises with age (at the end of the tax year).

Table 15.1 *How much you can pay into a personal pension contribution limits as a percentage of net relevant earnings for 1997/98*

Age on 6 April	% of pay	Maximum contribution
35 or less	17.5%	£14,700
36-45	20%	£16,800
46-50	25%	£21,000
51-55	30%	£25,200
56-60	35%	£29,400
61 or over	40%	£33,600

Table 15.2 *How much you can pay into a retirement annuity plan (these are pre-1 July 1988 personal pension plans and there is no earnings cap)*

Age on 6 April	% of pay
50 or less	17.5%
51–55	20.0%
56–60	22.5%
61 or over	27.5%

Tax tips:

- ☐ You can also pay 5 per cent of these contributions into a life insurance policy which pays out on death before 75. You can therefore get tax relief on life insurance contributions.
- ☐ Because there is no earnings cap on retirement annuities, higher earners who have existing (pre-1 July 1988) plans may find these better than personal pension plans even though the maximum contribution limits are lower.
- ☐ If you have an old-style retirement annuity and your salary is within the earnings cap (less than £84,000) and likely to remain so, consider taking out a personal pension scheme as the contribution limits are higher. Although you can have both a retirement annuity and a personal pension, you cannot get maximum tax relief on both. Ask for *Help Sheet IR330: Pension payments* for further information.

> **Tax warning**
>
> If you are lucky enough to have an employer who contributes to your personal pension plan, remember that the maximum contribution limits **include** employer contributions and **no** tax relief is given on employer's contributions.

HOW TAX RELIEF IS GIVEN

You can only make contributions out of *net relevant earnings* which means you can only pay pension contributions out of:

- any earnings from non-pensionable employment;
- profits from self-employment;
- your share of partnership profits;
- profits from furnished holiday lettings.

You cannot make contributions out of savings income.

If you are self-employed your pension contributions will reduce the level of your profits which are liable to tax. So if you pay in £10,000 of contributions, £10,000 of your profits will no longer be taxed. If you are a higher-rate taxpayer you will therefore save £4000 of tax. Your relief will be limited to a percentage of your *net relevant earnings* (see table 15.2).

If you are an employee paying into a personal pension, basic-rate tax relief of 23 per cent will automatically be invested in your pension because you pay your contributions *net* of tax relief.

For instance, if you pay in £77 a month £23 a month will be paid in by the Inland Revenue. If you contribute £100 a month this rises to £130 following tax relief. Any higher-rate tax relief will be calculated using your Tax Return and you will get a tax rebate and/or your Tax Code will be adjusted so that you receive higher-rate tax relief through your PAYE earnings. Even if you do **not** want to claim higher-rate relief you must **still** include pension contributions on your Tax Return.

HOW TO MAXIMIZE TAX RELIEF

If you have *net relevant earnings* in any year but do not pay the maximum permitted contributions, the difference between what

FILLING IN YOUR TAX RETURN

you actually contribute and what you could have paid is *unused tax relief*. This tax relief can be carried forward so you can use up this extra tax relief in future years. You can *carry forward* the unused allowance for the next six tax years. The unused relief will be in addition to the maximum relief for that year. Ask for *Help Sheet IR330: Pension payments*.

> **Tax tip**
>
> If you are **not** earning enough to pay 40 per cent tax but think you will next year or in future years, consider carrying forward some or all of your unused relief to a year when you can get tax relief at 40 per cent instead of 23 per cent.

You can also *carry back* pension contributions to get tax relief for a past tax year. You can only carry back premiums to the preceding tax year. But if you had **no** *net relevant earnings* in that year, you can carry back to the year before that. You can either do this using your Tax Return or making a separate election to your Tax Office by 31 January 1999. Ask for form *PP43* (or *43* if you have a retirement annuity).

> **Tax tip**
>
> If you are a basic-rate taxpayer this year but were a higher 40 per cent taxpayer last year and did not make maximum contributions last year, consider carrying back premiums so you can get tax relief at the higher rate.

You can also *bring back* contributions made after 5 April 1998 but before you send in your Tax Return. So if you make a pension contribution in June 1998 you can include it on your Tax Return for tax year to 5 April 1998 (the one you are now filling in) and claim tax relief a year earlier. If you have sent in your Tax Return before making the post-5 April 1998 contributions, you can make an election before waiting for your 5 April 1999 Tax Return.

If you want to carry back, carry forward or bring back payments or you have exceeded the appropriate percentage limits of your earnings ask for *Help Sheet IR330*. Doctors and dentists should ask for leaflet *IR1* from the Orderline.

Personal pension plans taken out before 1 July 1988 are called retirement annuity contracts. If you pay into both a retirement annuity contract and personal pension plan there are special rules. Ask for *Help Sheet IR330*.

TAX RELIEF

> **Tax tip**
>
> If you have paid in more than the percentage of earnings allowed ask for *Help Sheet IR330: Pension payments*.

THE SELF-EMPLOYED AND THOSE IN PARTNERSHIP

14 Do you want to claim relief for pension contributions?
Do not include contributions deducted from your pay by your employer to their pension scheme, because tax relief is given automatically. But do include your contributions to personal pension schemes.

NO ☐   YES ☐   If yes, fill in boxes 14.1 to 14.17 as appropriate.

- **Retirement annuity contracts**

Qualifying payments made in 1997-98	14.1 £	1997-98 payments used in an earlier year	14.2 £	Relief claimed
1997-98 payments now to be carried back	14.3 £	Payments brought back from 1998-99	14.4 £	box 14.1 minus (boxes 14.2 and 14.3, but not 14.4) 14.5 £

- *Self-employed contributions to personal pension plans*

Qualifying payments made in 1997-98	14.6 £	1997-98 payments used in an earlier year	14.7 £	Relief claimed
1997-98 payments now to be carried back	14.8 £	Payments brought back from 1998-99	14.9 £	box 14.6 minus (boxes 14.7 and 14.8, but not 14.9) 14.10 £

Note: Retirement annuity contracts are those taken out pre-1 July 1988. Personal pensions are contracts taken out after this date.

Boxes 14.1 and 14.6:

Enter the total contributions for the year.

Boxes 14.2 and 14.7:

If you made payments in the 1997/98 tax year but included these payments on a previous Tax Return (you carried them back to the last tax year and asked for this on your 1996/97 Tax Return) write in the amount here. The same applies if you have written to your Tax Office and asked for an election for payments to be carried back.

Boxes 14.3 and 14.8:

These are contributions you want to carry back to earlier years. As explained above, if you did not pay in the maximum allowed last year you can *carry back* a contribution made this year either to get higher-rate tax relief from a past year or so that you can pay in more than the maximum allowed this year.

FILLING IN YOUR TAX RETURN

Boxes 14.4 and 14.9:

This is for contributions made after the end of the tax year (after 5 April 1998) which you want to be classed as contributions for the tax year ending 5 April 1998.

Boxes 14.5 and 14.10:

Follow the simple sum on your Tax Return to arrive at the amount of relief you want to claim.

> **Tax tip**
>
> If you realize you are going to face a large tax bill for 1997/98 (the one covered by your Tax Return) and want to reduce it after the end of the tax year you can do this by making a pension contribution after 5 April but before you send in your Tax Return. Put the amount in the boxes 14.4, 14.9 or 14.14. Remember you can only do this if you did not contribute the maximum percentage of your net relevant earnings into a pension in the 1997/98 tax year.

Doctors and dentists whose NHS earnings are classed as self-employed profits should read the notes on page 20 of the Tax Return Guide.

Q15: OTHER TAX RELIEFS

📄 PAPERWORK REQUIRED

This will include:

- [ ] details of any vocational training costs you have incurred (NVQ or SVQ);
- [ ] details of any mortgages **not** in MIRAS. You should have a certificate of loan interest paid from your lender;
- [ ] interest payments on loans secured on your home to buy a life annuity if you are over 65 and this is **not** linked to a pension. These are also known as home income plans;
- [ ] interest details if you took out a loan to buy shares or fund a small company or partnership;

TAX RELIEF

- ☐ documentation covering all maintenance and alimony payments;
- ☐ subscriptions to venture capital trusts or enterprise investment schemes;
- ☐ amounts you have given to charities under Gift Aid or covenant;
- ☐ details of any expenses incurred in a business that has ceased (post cessation expenses);
- ☐ losses incurred on investing in any relevant discounted securities (deep discount bonds);
- ☐ payments made to a trade union or friendly society for death benefits.

Read page 20 of your Tax Return Guide which explains these reliefs and what you can claim.

• Payments you made for vocational training   Amount of payment 15.1 £

Box 15.1:

Tax relief is given to those who pay for their own vocational training provided this counts towards a National or Scottish Vocational Qualification. So even if you are only doing one of the five levels or 'units of competence' and are not studying for the full qualification, you can still get tax relief. However, any payments for GCSEs or A-level courses do **not** qualify for tax relief even when they are taken as a preliminary course to an NVQ or SVQ.

> **Tax tip**
>
> You can also get tax relief for training which does not involve NVQs or SVQs if it provides skills or knowledge which are relevant to – and intended to be used in – paid employment or self-employment. To qualify the course must be full-time for at least four consecutive weeks but for no more than a year and you must be aged 30 or over.

To qualify you must be:

- ☐ aged 16, 17 or 18 but not in full-time education at a school; or
- ☐ age 19 or over and paying for your own training; and

FILLING IN YOUR TAX RETURN

☐ not in receipt of any grants or assistance under a government scheme.

You will usually know if the scheme qualifies for tax relief as basic-rate tax relief is deducted from your fees before you pay them. So if the training costs are £400, you pay them after basic-rate tax is deducted. So you pay £400 – 23 per cent (£92) = £308. You save the basic-rate tax of £92 and this is your tax relief. Write the figure after tax relief in **Box 15.1**.

If you are a higher-rate taxpayer you can claim the further tax relief of 17 per cent (40 per cent less 23 per cent) by filling in **Box 15.1**. Ask for leaflet *IR119: Tax relief for vocational training* before filling in this box.

• Interest on loans to buy your main home (other than MIRAS)   Amount of payment 15.2 £

Box 15.2: mortgage interest

Mortgage interest relief on loans to buy your main home rarely has to be claimed as it is given automatically by most lenders under the MIRAS scheme with tax relief deducted from your mortgage payments. Relief is 15 per cent of the interest payments on the first £30,000 of a homeloan used to buy your only or main home. This was reduced to ten per cent from April 1998.

However, if your mortgage is **not** covered by MIRAS you **must** claim tax relief.

To work out the figure to write in **Box 15.2** ask for *Help Sheet IR340: Relief on loans not in MIRAS* and work through the sheet to get the amount you want to claim.

Tax tips:

☐ If you took out a loan to pay for home improvements before 6 April 1988 it would have qualified for tax relief (provided that when it was added to your other loans you came within the MIRAS threshold). This tax relief was scrapped on home improvement loans taken out after that date. So if you have a pre-6 April 1988 loan, think twice about repaying it or switching it to a cheaper loan. If you do, you will lose the tax relief.

☐ Mortgage interest relief is equally split on joint mortgages taken out by married couples. But if one partner is a non-taxpayer and your mortgage is not in MIRAS you could be wasting this relief. Elect to have the entire or bulk of the mortgage tax relief given to the partner who is a taxpayer. Remember this is only for loans that are not in MIRAS. You should fill in

TAX RELIEF

- Form 15 and have a year from the end of the tax year in which to make the change.
- ☐ If you marry each partner can continue to receive £30,000 tax relief on their individual properties for up to 12 months after the wedding and can also qualify for a further £30,000 of tax relief on a mortgage to buy a new marital home. This means that newly weds can get MIRAS on £90,000 of home loans – but for up to one year only.
- ☐ If you are moving home and have not been able to sell your existing property you can receive tax relief on both properties for up to one year. This tax relief is also available on bridging loans.
- ☐ If you expect to become a non-taxpayer in the future make sure your loan is in MIRAS as you will still qualify for tax relief even though you do not pay tax. If the loan is not in MIRAS you will have to make a separate claim for relief.
- ☐ Mortgage tax relief is not restricted to houses and flats, it can also apply to caravans and houseboats if these are your only or main home.
- ☐ If you took out a mortgage with another person before 1 August 1998 (and still have the same home loan) each buyer will qualify for £30,000 of tax relief. So if two of you bought the property you would have £60,000 of tax relief between you. Think twice before switching your loan as you will lose this relief and come under new rules which restrict mortgage tax relief to £30,000 per property instead of £30,000 per home buyer. The same applies if you marry but bought your home with your partner before 1 August 1998 – your tax relief will be halved when you wed.
- ☐ If you use part of your home for business you can treat the loan to buy your property as two separate loans and claim mortgage interest relief for the part relating to the residential use of the property but no mortgage interest relief on the proportion relating to business use. However, you can set the interest on the business proportion of the loan against your business profits. You must split the loan in proportion to the amount of the property used for business. Ask your Tax Office for advice.
- ☐ If you let more than a third of your home you should opt out of MIRAS, although you may still be able to claim tax relief directly and save even more tax. If you opt out you can claim a proportion of your mortgage interest (or all of the interest if your entire property is let) to reduce your rental profits and therefore tax. And instead of tax relief being restricted to 15 per cent of the first £30,000 you will save tax at the highest rate of tax you pay on all the allowable interest regardless of the size of the loan.

FILLING IN YOUR TAX RETURN

- Interest on other qualifying loans   Amount of payment 15.3 £

Box 15.3: tax relief on other loans

The qualifying loans included in this box are:

- ☐ Loans you take out to lend money to or buy shares in a company in which you either own 5 per cent of the share capital or own part of the share capital and are also an employee. These cover *close companies* and *employee controlled companies*.
- ☐ Loans to buy an interest in a trading or professional *partnership* or to buy plant or machinery for that partnership or to provide that partnership with capital **provided** your interest costs have not been included in the Partnership accounts or on the Partnership pages. Normally the interest payments are deducted from your profits before calculating tax. Loans for self-employment should already be included on the relevant pages as should loans to buy a property for let.
- ☐ Loans to buy shares in or lend money to a business cooperative.
- ☐ Loans to buy plant or machinery for use in your work for your employer.

You get tax relief on these loans at your top rate of tax.

Box 15.3 also covers interest on loans to buy *life annuities* for the over 65s which are also known as *home income plans*. The loan must be secured on your only or main home and the borrower or person who receives the annuity must be 65 or over when the loan is made.

These schemes are a way for the elderly to receive an income from the cash tied up in their property. They take out a loan secured on their home and buy an annuity which then covers the interest payments on the loan and gives them a regular income.

Tax relief is given at the **basic-rate of tax**, 23 per cent, and is **not** restricted to 15 per cent like mortgage tax relief.

If you have one of these plans ask for *Help Sheet IR340: Relief for loans not in MIRAS*.

> **Tax tip**
>
> You may also be able to claim relief for any low-interest or interest-free loans from your employer if you have been taxed on these as an employee benefit. Ask for Help Sheet *IR145: Low-interest loans provided by employers.*

TAX RELIEF

- Maintenance or alimony payments you have made under a court order, Child Support Agency assessment or legally binding order or agreement

  Amount claimed under 'new' rules
  15.4 £

  Amount claimed under 'old' rules up to £1,830
  15.5 £

  Amount claimed under 'old' rules over £1,830
  15.6 £

Boxes 15.4, 15.5 and 15.6: Maintenance or alimony payments

Tax relief is given on payments to a spouse or former spouse or child following divorce or under a verbal or written separation agreement, court order or Child Support Agency assessment.

You **cannot** get tax relief for other payments including voluntary payments or payments made to your children if they are aged 21 or over.

You cannot claim the maintenance tax relief on lump sums as part of a divorce settlement even if these are paid in instalments. And if you pay your former spouse's mortgage and get mortgage tax relief you cannot claim tax relief again. Any other bills covered by the court order or legal agreement count towards the £1830 limit.

Tax relief varies depending on whether you have an *existing obligation* covered by the 'old rules' or not.

The 'old rules' apply if:

☐ maintenance payments were agreed or made by court order **before 15 March 1988**, or a court order made by 30 June 1988 which was applied for on or before 15 March 1988; or

☐ if you make maintenance payments under a written agreement or deed which was made before 15 March 1988 or submitted to your Inspector of Taxes by 30 June 1988.

If the 'old rules' apply you fill in **Box 15.5**. But do not simply write in the amount of maintenance you paid. You must first compare the amount of maintenance you paid in the April 1997 to April 1998 tax year with the amount on which you received tax relief in the 1988 to 1989 tax year. You must use the **smaller** of these two figures.

So if you paid £2000 maintenance in 1997/98 and £1800 maintenance in 1988/89 the figure you must write in **Box 15.5** will be £1800.

However, the tax relief on the first £1830 of payments is restricted to 15 per cent.

So if you paid £3000 of maintenance in both 1997/98 and in 1988/89 the figure you must write in **Box 15.5** will be £1830. The figure will either be £1830 or the amount you paid in maintenance (the smaller of the 1997/98 and 1988/89 figures), whichever is the lower.

FILLING IN YOUR TAX RETURN

Any maintenance payments above this £1830 threshold qualify for tax relief at your highest rate of tax. So, to follow the example above, in **Box 15.6** you should write £3000 − £1830 = £1170.

You can get tax relief if you pay maintenance directly to a child but you only get tax relief on the amount of maintenance you paid which qualified for tax relief in 1988/89.

If you have to pay maintenance payments to more than one former spouse you can get tax relief on both under the 'old rules'. This is the sum of the lower of the two amounts for each agreement.

If the court order was made on or after **15 March 1998** 'new rules' apply and you can only get tax relief up to the £1830 limit with this relief restricted to 15 per cent. There is no additional tax relief unlike under the 'old rules'.

So in **Box 15.4** you must write either £1830 or the amount of maintenance you paid if this is lower.

If you make two lots of maintenance payments, one under the 'old rules' and one under the 'new rules', you can get tax relief under both sets of rules. The tax relief under the new rules is only given if the figure in **Box 15.5** is less than £1830. Subtract the figure in **Box 15.5** from £1830 and enter in **Box 15.4** the lower of:

- that figure; and
- the amount you paid in 1997/98 under your new rules arrangement.

> **Tax tips:**
>
> - If you paid more in maintenance in 1997/98 than in 1988/89 you may be better off electing for the 'new rules' to apply but only if you currently pay less than £1830 a year in maintenance. By switching you can claim tax relief on today's higher amount of maintenance payments. This is because any increases in your maintenance payments are not taken into account under the 'old rules'. You must make the election within 12 months of the end of the tax year and write to inform the person to whom you pay maintenance. Once you have switched to the new system you cannot change back.
> - Do not elect to switch from the 'old rules' if you make payments directly to a child as they do not qualify for tax relief under the 'new rules'.
> - If your maintenance payments are above £1830 – and were above this in 1988/89 – you will be better off under the 'old rules' so be careful not to change any arrangement as the 'new rules' will apply.
> - You cannot get tax relief for payments made directly to a child under the

TAX RELIEF

> 'new rules' so ensure that any agreements specify that payments are made to your former spouse.
>
> ☐ Any voluntary maintenance payments you make do not qualify for tax relief. Only enforceable maintenance arrangements made under a court order, a legally-binding written agreement or under an assessment by the Child Support Agency qualify for tax relief. So ensure you have a legal agreement.
>
> ☐ Only if the spouse has not remarried (or is unlikely to) will you be better under the 'new rules' as once your former spouse remarries you lose all tax relief. So if your former spouse is likely to remarry do not switch to the new rules.

Note: Tax relief can either be given through your PAYE Tax Code or a lower tax bill/tax rebate by filling in a Tax Return or informing your tax office.

> **IMPORTANT:** You must give details including dates and details of the type of agreement or court order in the 'Additional information' box on page 8 of your Tax Return.

For more information ask for *Help Sheet IR93: Separation, divorce and maintenance payments.*

- Subscriptions for Venture Capital Trust shares (up to £100,000)
  Amount on which relief claimed **15.7** £ _____

- Subscriptions under the Enterprise Investment Scheme (up to £100,000)
  Amount on which relief claimed **15.8** £ _____

Boxes 15.7 and 15.8: Venture Capital Trusts and Enterprise Investment Schemes

These offer tax breaks **when you invest** so they are a good way to reduce your tax bill quickly. However, the risks can be high. Tax relief of 20 per cent is given on investments up to £100,000, giving a maximum tax relief of £20,000. The investment limit increased to £150,000 from 6 April 1998.

Venture capital trusts are funds which in turn invest in growing businesses. You must hold the shares for a minimum of five years. Any dividends paid out by the trust or gains you make when you sell the shares in the trust are also tax free. Enterprise Investment schemes also encourage investment in small unquoted companies.

FILLING IN YOUR TAX RETURN

> **Tax tip**
>
> Not only do you receive generous tax relief on these schemes but if you are reinvesting the gain made from selling another investment or asset you can claim what is called capital gains reinvestment relief. This means that you do not have to pay any Capital Gains Tax until you dispose of your shares in the venture capital trust or EIS Scheme.

If you have invested in an enterprise investment scheme you **must** have either form *EIS3* or *EIS5* to fill in this section. Do not fill in this Box until you receive the form. You must also include any investments during the tax year for which you have already received relief in your Tax Code (your PAYE tax has been altered to give you tax relief already).

You must write details of each EIS investment in the 'Additional information' box on page 8 of your Tax Return.

> **Tax tip**
>
> If you invest in an EIS before 6 October 1998 you can ask for half of this investment up to a maximum of £15,000 to be deducted from your income for the 1997/98 tax year (the one covered by this Tax Return) to reduce your tax bill for the tax year before you made the investment. So you can effectively reduce your tax liability retrospectively.

- Charitable covenants or annuities   15.9 £
- Gift Aid   15.10 £

Boxes 15.9 and 15.10: Charitable payments

Two types of charitable payments qualify for tax relief. Charitable covenants are legally binding agreements to pay a certain amount to charity for more than three years. Gift Aid donations must be at least £250 and made in cash.

Both are ways for you to give to charity in a tax-efficient manner. In both cases basic-tax relief of 23 per cent is given automatically as the charity can recover this from the Inland Revenue.

So for every £77 you pay in the charity reclaims £23 tax relief. Or if you pay in £100 the charity can claim £30 bringing the total donation up to £130.

However, if you are a higher-rate taxpayer **you** not the charity claim the higher-rate tax relief. The extra tax relief is the difference between the higher-rate and basic-rate of tax (40 per cent – 23 per cent = 17 per cent). You claim this higher-rate relief on your Tax Return. So as a higher-rate taxpayer on a £100 donation you will get 17 per cent tax relief = £17.

Although basic-tax relief is claimed by the charity do **not** gross up the amounts paid to take this into account. Simply add up the total payments made during the tax year.

> **Tax tips:**
>
> ☐ Even if you are not a higher-rate taxpayer (and as such cannot claim tax relief on your charitable donations) consider making all charity payments either through covenants or Gift Aid as the charity can then receive more by claiming basic-rate tax on what you donate.
> ☐ Using a covenant to give to charity can have its benefits. For instance, if you donate to the National Trust or another charitable body you may receive free or reduced-priced entry to the charity's properties.
> ☐ If you are married and want to make charitable donations through a covenant or Gift Aid, make sure that the partner who is the higher-rate taxpayer makes the payment – that way you can claim higher-rate tax relief.

- Post-cessation expenses and losses on relevant discounted securities etc.　**15.11** £

Box 15.11: Post cessation expenses

This box is for those who used to run a business and incurred expenses related to that business after it ceases. You can get relief for these expenses if they are spent:

☐ remedying or paying damages for defective work or goods or services;
☐ on legal or other professional services in connection with any claim that the work, goods or services were defective;
☐ on insurance against any of the above expenses; or
☐ in recovering debts which have been taken into account in calculating the business profits before it ceased.

In addition you can claim relief for debts owed to the business which have been taken into account in calculating your profits or

FILLING IN YOUR TAX RETURN

gains before your business ceased provided this is done within seven years. See page 22 of the Tax Return Guide for further information.

- Payments to a trade union or friendly society for death benefits

Half amount of payment
15.12 £

Box 15.12: Trade union and friendly society payments for death benefits

This is a tax relief that few people know about. You can claim tax relief for:

- ☐ the part of your trade union subscription that pays for a pension (superannuation), life assurance or funeral benefits;
- ☐ the part of any friendly society premiums paid to provide sickness and death benefits provided the premium is **no** more than £25 per month **and** 40 per cent or less of the premiums is charged for the death benefit.

But you do not get tax relief on all of the amount. Find out from your trade union or friendly society how much of your premium provides the pension, life assurance, funeral or death benefit. Then divide this amount by **half** and write this figure in **Box 15.12**. This is because tax relief is only given on one half of the amount you pay.

> **Tax tips:**
>
> ☐ If you have an option to pay for life insurance or death benefits through a trade union or friendly society, take the offer up as this is one of the only ways you can get tax relief on your payments. The other is buying life insurance through your pension.
>
> ☐ Always check with your trade union or friendly society to see if tax relief is available as you may be unaware that you can claim this relief.

16

TAX ALLOWANCES

Tax allowances are explained in greater detail in Part 2 of this book which you should read to understand how allowances, allowance restrictions and earnings restrictions affect your tax bill. **It is important you understand how allowances work as they are one of the easiest ways to reduce your tax bill.**

📄 PAPERWORK REQUIRED

This will include:

- PAYE Coding Notices (if you have received these) telling you what allowances you are already claiming/receiving;
- details of any registration with a local authority if you are registered blind;
- marriage details (dates);
- any correspondence from the Inland Revenue about tax allowances.

> **Tax tip**
>
> Even if you have forgotten to claim a tax allowance for a previous tax year, you can still make a tax saving. This is because you can go back six years to claim an allowance you did not know you were entitled to. Tax relief will be given at the rate of tax which would have applied at that time.

Q16: ALLOWANCES

Q16 — You get your personal allowance of £4,045 automatically. **If you were born before 6 April 1933, enter your date of birth in box 21.4** - you may get higher age-related allowances.

Do you want to claim any of the following allowances? NO ☐ YES ☐

If yes, please read pages 23 to 26 of your Tax Return Guide and then fill in boxes 16.1 to 16.28 as appropriate.

FILLING IN YOUR TAX RETURN

It is important that you read through all the questions before ticking the *YES* or *NO* box at the top of page 6.

You should only tick the *NO* box if:

☐ you are not married and were not married during the tax year;
☐ you are not a single parent/do not have a dependant child living with you;
☐ you were not widowed during the tax year or the year earlier;
☐ you are not registered blind;
☐ you have not been receiving the transitional allowance for married women with husband's on low income; and
☐ you do not want to transfer surplus allowances to your spouse (see the section on **Boxes 16.25** to **16.28** for more details).

Note: Even if you tick the *NO* box you should still read the Tax Tips at the end of this section as you may find that you can claim an allowance for a previous year or in a future year.

Please note that you do **not** have to claim the basic personal allowance. This is the allowance automatically given to everyone (apart from non-residents). The allowance for the 1997/98 tax year (the one covered by your Tax Return) is £4045. The allowance means that you do **not** pay tax on the first £4045 of income you earn.

Special rules for those aged 65 or over

The personal allowance rises with age. Those aged 65 or over during the tax year get an increased personal allowance of £5220 and those aged 75 or over an increased age allowance of £5400. As with the personal allowance, you do **not** need to claim these age-related allowances. The married couple's allowance also rises with age. To qualify for higher age-related allowances you – or your spouse in the case of the married couple's allowance – must have reached 65 or 75 on or before 5 April 1998. However, if your income is £15,600 or more, your allowances will be reduced. See the calculation on page 6 of Part 1 of this book.

■ *Blind person's allowance* Date of registration (if first year of claim) 16.1 / /   Local authority (or other register) 16.2

TAX ALLOWANCES

Boxes 16.1 and 16.2: Blind person's allowance

Allowance: £1280.

You can only claim this if you were registered blind with a local authority. Write the name of this authority in **Box 16.2**.

Only fill in **Box 16.1** if this is your first year of claiming. Note that you can still get the allowance for the year ended 5 April 1998 even if you had not registered as blind but provided you already had evidence of blindness at that date (usually an ophthalmologist's certificate).

Note that if you live in Scotland or Northern Ireland you can also claim the allowance if you are not able to perform any work for which eyesight is essential. Write 'Scotland Claim' or 'Northern Ireland claim' in **Box 16.2** if this is the case.

- Tick to claim and give details in the 'Additional information' box on page 8 (please see page 23 of your Tax Return Guide for what is needed)
- If you want to calculate your tax, enter the amount of transitional allowance you can have in box 16.4

Boxes 16.3 and 16.4: Transitional allowance

Allowance: Amount agreed with husband or his personal allowance of £4045 less his income during the tax year.

This can only be claimed by married women who were in receipt of the transitional allowance in the 1996/97 tax year.

It is given to some wives with husbands on low income. To meet the requirements they must:

☐ still be living with the same husband as in the whole of the 1996/97 tax year;
☐ be married to a husband who was resident in the UK during the tax year; and
☐ the husband must have written to his Tax Office asking for the allowance to be given to the wife.

To claim the wife must tick **Box 16.3** and give details of her husband's name, address, tax reference, National Insurance number and Tax Office in the 'Additional information' box on page 8 of the Tax Return.

Only fill in **Box 16.4** if you want to calculate your own tax liability. If you do, write in the amount of allowance agreed with

FILLING IN YOUR TAX RETURN

your husband or ask your Tax Office for the figure to put in the box.

- **Married couple's allowance for a married man** - see page 23 of your Tax Return Guide.

- Wife's full name **16.5**
- Wife's date of birth (if before 6 April 1933) **16.7** / /
- Wife's tax reference (if known, please) **16.9**
- Date of marriage (if after 5 April 1997) **16.6** / /
- Tick box 16.8 if you or your wife have allocated half the allowance to her **16.8**
- Tick box 16.10 if you and your wife have allocated all the allowance to her **16.10**

Married and separated men: married couple's allowance

Allowance: £1830 (with the amount of tax relief restricted to 15 per cent giving a maximum tax saving of £275). This allowance rises with age to £3185 (also restricted to 15 per cent) if one spouse is aged 65 or over during the tax year and to £3225 (also restricted to 15 per cent tax relief) if one spouse is aged 75 or over during the tax year. The rate of relief will fall to ten per cent from 1999.

Only fill these boxes in if you are:

☐ a married man (women need to fill in **Boxes 16.11** to **16.15**);
☐ or were a married man during the tax year but are now separated from your wife.

> **Tax tip**
>
> Even if you were separated from your wife before 6 April 1991 but you were still married to her on 6 April 1997 and have wholly maintained her since separation until at least 6 April 1997 with voluntary payments for which you were not entitled to tax relief, you may still be able to claim the married couple's allowance.

Tax rules state that you must be 'living' with your wife. However, this does not mean you have to live under the same roof, only that you are still married and neither of you intends to make the separation permanent.

Boxes 16.5, 16.7 and 16.9:

Write your wife's full name, her date of birth (if before 6 April 1933 so that you can claim any higher age-related married couple's

TAX ALLOWANCES

allowance) and her tax reference number if you have this.

Box 16.6:

Write your date of marriage if it was after 5 April 1997.

Special rules for newly weds

If you married during the tax year (between 6 April 1997 and 5 April 1998) you may not be able to claim the full married couple's allowance. The tax relief is given for every month of marriage during the tax year and is reduced by each complete tax month (from 6th of one month to the 5th of the next) which has passed before the wedding.

So if you marry on 1 July, the complete tax months of April, May and June do not qualify for married couple's allowance. So that is three months out of 12 so your allowance of £1830 will be reduced by 3/12 = £1373.

> **Tax tips:**
>
> ☐ You should not claim the married couple's allowance for your new marriage if you were entitled to the full married couple's allowance from a previous marriage. This is because you can claim the married couple's allowance for the whole year – not just for the part of the year in which you remarried. If you do not want to claim the married couple's allowance for your new marriage do not fill in Box 16.6 but simply fill in the boxes with your previous wife's details.
>
> ☐ You should not claim the married couple's allowance if you are entitled to claim the additional personal allowance because you have a child living with you. This is because you can claim the entire additional personal allowance (which is the same as the married couple's allowance) but can only claim the married couple's allowance from the date you married. Note, you cannot claim the additional personal allowance and the married couple's allowance. If you want to claim the additional personal allowance do not fill in Boxes 16.5 to 16.10. Fill in Boxes 16.16 to 16.23 instead.

Boxes 16.8 and 16.10: Allocating all or half of the allowance to your wife

Your wife can ask for half of the married couple's allowance to be offset against her tax – without your permission. However, she

FILLING IN YOUR TAX RETURN

must do this by the start of the relevant tax year – so this cannot be backdated.

If she wants to claim the whole allowance, she needs your permission as this must be a joint election. Again this must be done by the start of the tax year. So if you make an election now, it will not apply until 6 April 1999. However, if you married during the 1997/98 tax year and made an election by 5 April 1998 this will apply for the 1997/98 tax year.

This election will remain until it is revoked.

You must make an election by notifying your (or her) Tax Office in writing. Ask for form 180.

Special rules for those aged 65 or over

Although you can alter the way the married couple's allowance is given, you can only split the basic married couple's allowance of £1830. The remainder of the higher age-related married couple's allowance must always be given to the husband. So if you qualify for a married couple's allowance of £3185, only the first £1830 can be given to the wife – the remaining £1355 must still be given to the husband.

However, if you cannot use up your allowance (because you do not have sufficient income) you can transfer any surplus allowance to your wife. For instance, if you have an income of £6000 and are over 65 you will have allowances of £8403 (£5220 basic plus the £3185 married couples allowance). You will have £2405 of unused allowances. The first £1830 of married couples allowance can go to your wife. The remaining surplus of £575 can be transferred by filling in **Boxes 16.25** to **16.28**.

> **Tax warning:** Although you can claim the higher age-related allowances if you or your wife were aged 65 or over during the tax year (on or before 5 April 1998) these allowances will be reduced if your income was over £15,600 for the tax year.
>
> Your allowances will be reduced by £1 for every £2 of income over £15,600. So if you have income of more than £19,600 you will exceed this earnings restriction by £4000. So your allowances will be reduced by £2000 (£1 for every £2 of income). Your personal allowance will be reduced first. However, your age-related personal allowance cannot be reduced to less than the basic personal allowance of £4045.
>
> So if you are 65, have an age-related personal allowance of £5220, and have income of £19,600 (as in the example above) your allowance should be

TAX ALLOWANCES

> reduced to £3220 (£5220 – £2000. As this is below £4045 you will be given a basic personal allowance of £4045 and the remainder of the reduction (£4045 – £3220= £825) will be used to reduce your married couple's allowance. As you are over 65 this is £3185. So £3185 – £825 = £2360. Once again, your age-related married couple's allowance cannot be reduced to less than the basic married couple's allowance of £1830. For further explanation see the allowances section in Part 1, Chapter 1.

> **Tax tip**
>
> If you are claiming the age allowance and earn more than £15,600 you may benefit from switching some of your income to your wife (but you have to give it to her as an outright gift and it must be in her name). This is because you lose £1 of age-related allowance for every £2 of income over £15,600. You will lose all of the extra age-related personal and married couple's allowances if you have an income of more than £20,660 (if you are both aged over 65 but under 75). By switching your income to your wife, you can reduce your income and as such the reduction in your age allowances.

■ *Married couple's allowance for a married woman - see page 24 of your Tax Return Guide.*

- Date of marriage (if after 5 April 1997)   16.11
- Husband's full name   16.12
- Tick box 16.13 if you or your husband have allocated half the allowance to you   16.13
- Husband's tax reference (if known, please)   16.14
- Tick box 16.15 if you and your husband have allocated all the allowance to you   16.15

Married and separated women: married couple's allowance

Even if you are married, or were married, during the tax year you may not have to fill in this section. You should only fill it in if:

☐ you have agreed with your Tax Office that you can claim **half** of the married couple's allowance;
☐ you have agreed with your **husband** and your Tax Office that you can claim **all** of the married couple's allowance.

You can only make a claim if you were married and living with your husband (or living apart but with no intention to separate) for all or part of the tax year ended 5 April 1998.

Box 16.11:

Only fill this in if you married after 5 April 1997.

Boxes 16.12 and 16.14:

Write your husband's full name and his tax reference if you know this.

> **Tax tips:**
>
> ☐ Do not fill in Box 16.11 if you are still entitled to claim half or all of the married couple's allowance from a previous marriage. This is because you will only be able to claim all or half the married couple's allowance for your new marriage from the date you married. If you continue to make the claim for your old marriage you can claim your share of the married couple's allowance for the whole tax year. This will only usually apply if you were married then quickly divorce and remarry.
>
> ☐ Do not fill in Box 16.11 if you were entitled to claim the additional personal allowance (which is the same as the married couple's allowance) because you were unmarried and had a child living with you before you married during the tax year. This is because you can claim the additional personal allowance for the entire tax year, but can only claim all (or your share) of the married couple's allowance from the date you married.

Boxes 16.13 and 16.15:

The married couple's allowance automatically goes to the husband. Although the wife can claim half the allowance **without** his consent, she **must** agree this with her Tax Office **before** the start of the tax year. However, if you married during the tax year you can make the election to split the married couple's allowance for the first year of marriage provided you do this by the end of the tax year.

> **Tax tip**
>
> If your husband has insufficient income to use up his allowances (his income is less than his allowances) you can claim his surplus allowances. Fill in Boxes 16.25 to 16.28.

Special rules for those newly-widowed

If your husband died during the tax year ended 5 April 1998, you can claim any part of the married couple's allowance which could

TAX ALLOWANCES

not be offset against his income. So for this to apply, his income must have been less than the married couple's allowance. This applies even if you had previously agreed that you would claim all or half of the married couple's allowance.

Married men and women

> **Tax tip:**
>
> Now that the married couple's allowance is restricted to 15 per cent tax relief there is no point in switching it from husband to wife if the wife is a higher-rate taxpayer and the husband a basic-rate taxpayer. However, if the husband is a non-earner he should switch all of his allowance to his wife so she can benefit from the 15 per cent tax relief on £1830 of earnings = £275.

■ Additional personal allowance (available in some circumstances if you have a child living with you - see page 24 of your Tax Return Guide).

- Name of the child claimed for   16.16
- Child's date of birth   16.17 / /
- Tick if child lives with you   16.18
- Name of university etc/type of training if the child is 16 or over on 6 April 1997 and in full time education or training   16.19

Those with a dependant child living with them: Additional Personal Allowance

Allowance: £1830 restricted to 15 per cent tax relief (giving a tax saving of £275).

Many people do not know that they can claim this allowance which as such can be overlooked. However, even if you have forgotten to claim in the past remember you can backdate your claim for six years.

You can claim the allowance if you are unmarried, separated, divorced or widowed throughout the tax year **and** have a dependant child living with you.

You can claim this allowance even if the child only lives with you for part of the year. If the child lives with both you and your former spouse or partner you can split the allowance.

Rules for women

You can still claim the allowances even if you married or were reconciled with your husband during the tax year ended 5 April 1998 provided the child lived with you for the part of the year in which you were single, separated, divorced or widowed. (See the section for women above on the married couple's allowance for Tax Tips.)

Rules for men

You can also claim the allowance if you separated permanently from your wife in the year ended 5 April 1998 but a child lived with you after you separated **and** you are not getting all the married couple's allowance. You can also claim the allowance if you married during the tax year (either remarried or married the mother of the child) and decided to claim this additional personal allowance instead of the married couple's allowance. (See the section for men above on the married couple's allowance for Tax Tips.)

Note: You cannot claim the full married couple's allowance and the full additional personal allowance if you separate during the year. The maximum you can get is the **lower of:**

- the share of the additional personal allowance you are entitled to when the full amount is shared with someone else; **or**
- the full amount of additional personal allowance **after** deducting any share of the married couple's allowance you may be entitled to.

Married men and now married women get an extra concession if their wife/husband was unable to look after herself/himself at all because of illness or disablement for the **whole** of the tax year. They can claim the full additional personal allowance and the full married couple's allowance.

Married men who separated from their wives before 6 April 1991 who are still entitled to married couple's allowance from that marriage cannot get any additional personal allowance.

To qualify for the allowance the child must:

- be your own child, a stepchild, legitimated child or a child you legally adopted before he or she was 18;
- be under 16 on 6 April 1997 and who you look after at your own expense;
- be over 16 but under 18 on 6 April 1997 **and** either in full-time education at school, college or university or receiving full-time training for at least two years for a trade or profession.

Note: You can only get one allowance even if more than one child lives with you.

TAX ALLOWANCES

Boxes 16.16 and 16.17:

Write in the name of the child claimed for and the child's date of birth. If you are claiming for more than one child, you must always write the name and age of the **youngest** child unless someone else is claiming for that child.

Box 16.18:

Tick this box if the child lives with you (even if for only part of the year).

Box 16.19:

If the child was 16 or over on 6 April 1997 (but under 18) write in the name of the university, school or college or the full-time training scheme the child attends.

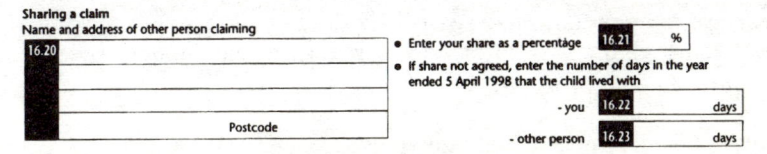

Boxes 16.20 to 16.23:

These boxes are for those sharing a claim. For example, a divorced couple may share custody of their children and can therefore share the allowance.

Write the name and address of the other person in **Box 16.20**.

If you have agreed a set share of the allowance write this in **Box 16.21**. You must use a percentage. So if you can claim two-thirds of the allowance write 67.

If you have not agreed a split, write the number of days the child lived with you in **Box 16.22** and the number of days the child lived with the other person in **Box 16.23**.

> **Tax tips:**
>
> ☐ If you are not married, but live together as husband and wife, you can only claim one allowance (for the youngest child) between you however many children you have. However, you can split the allowance so you get half each.

FILLING IN YOUR TAX RETURN

> ☐ If you are not living together as husband and wife and both look after more than one child, one of you may be able to claim for a different child instead of both claiming for the youngest. So you both get the full amount of allowance and do not have to split the allowance.

■ *Widow's bereavement allowance* • Date of your husband's death 16.24 / /

Box 16.24: Widow's bereavement allowance

Allowance: £1830 restricted to 15 per cent tax relief (giving a tax saving of £275).

This allowance is given in the year of your husband's death and, provided you do not remarry before the beginning of the following tax year, for the year following your husband's death. So if you were widowed during the tax year or your husband died in the previous tax year ending 5 April 1997 (and you did not remarry in that year) claim this allowance by writing the date of your husband's death in **Box 16.24**.

Note: This allowance is only given to widows, **not** widowers.

> **Tax tip:**
>
> If in the year of your husband's death he had insufficient income to use up the married couple's allowance the 'unused' surplus will automatically be passed to you as the widow. You do not have to make an election. However, if all or part of the married couple's allowance was transferred to you the widow by election before your husband's death, that married couple's allowance will be transferred back to the husband.

■ *Transfer of surplus allowances* - see page 25 of your Tax Return Guide before you fill in boxes 16.25 to 16.28.

• Tick if you want your spouse to have your unused allowances 16.25   • Tick if you want to have your spouse's unused allowances 16.26

Please give details in the 'Additional Information' box on page 8 - see page 25 of your Tax Return Guide for what is needed.

Boxes 16.25 to 16.28: Transfer of surplus allowances

This section may appear to be a little technical but it is worth understanding how you can save tax by transferring *surplus* or *unused allowances*.

Only those who are married and do not earn the total of all their

TAX ALLOWANCES

allowances can benefit. So if your income in the tax year was £4000 and your allowances were £5875 (£4045 for the basic allowance and £1830 for the married couple's allowance) you will have *unused* allowances that have not been used to reduce your taxable income. Remember allowances can only reduce your taxable income to zero – any unused amount of allowance is not then used to give you a tax rebate.

The only **unused** allowances that can be transferred are the married couple's allowance and the blind person's allowance. Although if you are a husband whose income does not use up all of the personal allowance **and** your wife received the transitional allowance in 1995/96 you may, in certain circumstances, be able to transfer unused personal allowances to her.

You must have lived with your spouse for at least part of the tax year in order to transfer any unused allowance.

If you want to transfer any surplus married couple's or blind person's allowance or the transitional allowance tick **Box 16.25**. If you are unsure if you will have any unused allowances add up your income and then add up your allowances. If your income is roughly equal to or less than the amount of allowances you think you are entitled to, tick the box. Your Tax Office will then work out the surplus.

Likewise, if you think your spouse's income will be less than their allowances, you can ask for these unused allowances to be transferred and used to reduce your tax bill. You can do this by ticking **Box 16.26**.

Note: If you tick **Box 16.25** or **16.26** you **must** then write your spouse's name, address, tax reference, National Insurance number and Tax Office in the 'Additional information' box on page 8 of your Tax Return.

17

TAX REFUNDS, CALCULATIONS AND OTHER INFORMATION

Q17: TAX REFUNDS

📄 PAPERWORK REQUIRED

This will include:

- ☐ correspondence from your Tax Office detailing any refund (a cheque should have been enclosed);
- ☐ correspondence from the Department of Social Security or Benefits Agency giving you a tax refund.

Have you already had any 1997-98 tax refunded or set off by your Tax Office or the DSS Benefits Agency? *Read the notes for box 17.1 on page 26 of your Tax Return Guide* NO YES If yes, enter the amount of the refund in box 17.1. 17.1 £

Note this question only applies to those who received a refund directly and does not cover tax refunds given through your PAYE code.

The tax refunded can include PAYE or SC60 tax or tax refunds on dividends, interest or other investment income.

You must also include any tax repayments which were not refunded to you but reallocated to other tax liabilities.

Write the amount of the tax refund in **Box 17.1**.

TAX REFUNDS, CALCULATIONS, OTHER INFORMATION

Q18: DO YOU WANT TO CALCULATE YOUR OWN TAX

📄 PAPERWORK REQUIRED

This will include:

- [ ] copies of any Notice of Tax Coding which detail any additional taxes you have paid;
- [ ] details of any payments 'on account' – tax you have already paid in advance for the 1997/98 tax year;
- [ ] a copy of the Inland Revenue Tax Calculation Guide.

Remember, calculating your tax bill is optional. You are strongly advised to tick the *NO* box. The Inland Revenue will then work out your tax for you. As such you will save on time and effort in completing the complex calculation and reduce the risks of making an error. However, you can **only** tick the *NO* box if you complete and return your Tax Return by **30 September 1998**. If you tick the *NO* box you do **not** have to fill in **Boxes 18.1 to 18.9**.

Even if you are employing a tax adviser or accountant to calculate your tax you must tick the *YES* box. And if you miss the 30 September 1998 deadline for sending back your Tax Return, you must also tick the *YES* box and then work through the complex calculations in your tax calculation guide.

Remember, if you tick the *YES* box you **must** then complete the Tax Calculation Guide and **Boxes 18.1 to 18.9**.

Boxes 18.6 to 18.8: Payments on account

Note that if you calculate your own tax (or get an accountant to do this for you) you must also calculate your first payment on account – the first interim tax payment for the 1998/99 tax year. This is due at the same time as your final balancing payment for the 1997/98 tax year. So on 31 January 1999 you will have two tax bills to pay.

Your payment on account is usually half the Income Tax and Class 4 NIC liability for the previous tax year. A second payment on account is due on 31 July 1999 and any outstanding tax will be paid the following 31 January.

FILLING IN YOUR TAX RETURN

However, you can ask for your payments on account to be reduced if your profits will be lower in the 1998/99 tax year. But do not ask for a reduction simply to cut down on advance tax payments. You can only take up this option if you reasonably expect profits to be lower. If your profits turn out to be higher than expected, you should inform your Tax Office as soon as possible. Note that if you reduce your payments on account by too much, you will be charged interest on the difference between what you should have paid and what you actually paid.

You only need to tick **Box 18.8** if your payments on account will be below £500 or most (80 per cent) of your income is taxed at source.

Q19: REPAYMENTS OF TAX

PAPERWORK REQUIRED

This will include:

☐ details of your accountant or tax adviser;
☐ your bank/building society details.

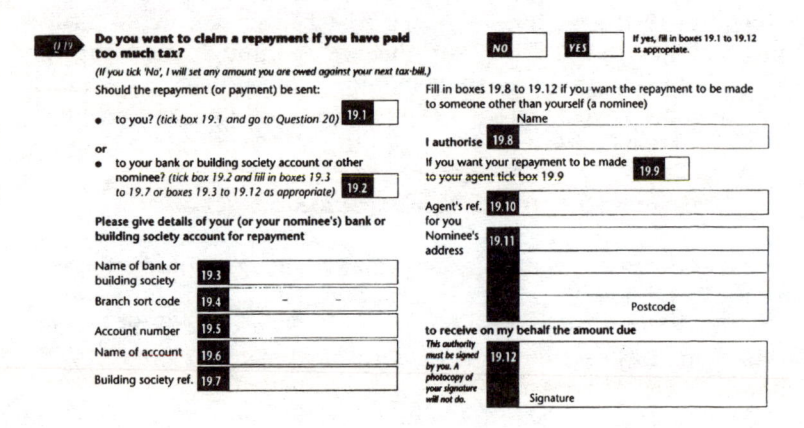

Q19 Do you want to claim a repayment if you have paid too much tax?
(If you tick 'No', I will set any amount you are owed against your next tax-bill.)
Should the repayment (or payment) be sent:
- to you? *(tick box 19.1 and go to Question 20)* **19.1**

or
- to your bank or building society account or other nominee? *(tick box 19.2 and fill in boxes 19.3 to 19.7 or boxes 19.3 to 19.12 as appropriate)* **19.2**

Please give details of your (or your nominee's) bank or building society account for repayment

Name of bank or building society	**19.3**
Branch sort code	**19.4** - -
Account number	**19.5**
Name of account	**19.6**
Building society ref.	**19.7**

NO ☐ YES ☐ *If yes, fill in boxes 19.1 to 19.12 as appropriate.*

Fill in boxes 19.8 to 19.12 if you want the repayment to be made to someone other than yourself (a nominee)
Name
I authorise **19.8**
If you want your repayment to be made to your agent tick box 19.9 **19.9**
Agent's ref. **19.10**
for you
Nominee's **19.11**
address

Postcode

to receive on my behalf the amount due
This authority must be signed by you. A photocopy of your signature will not do. **19.12**
Signature

This box simply tells the Inland Revenue that you want to have any tax paid to you (or your accountant or other tax adviser) rather than being offset against your next tax bill.

164

TAX REFUNDS, CALCULATIONS, OTHER INFORMATION

If you are also an employee and tick the *NO* box and owe less than £1000 in tax, your tax code will be adjusted so that you either have **less** tax deducted through PAYE (Pay-As-You-Earn – the system under which tax is deducted from employees pay).

You can tick the *YES* box even if you are unsure whether or not you are due a tax repayment.

Either tick **Box 19.1** and leave the rest of **Q19** blank. This will be the case if you want the repayment sent to the address on the front of your Tax Return.

Or tick **Box 19.2** and fill in the rest of the boxes. This will be the case if you want any refund paid directly into your bank or building society account or for the repayment to go to your *agent* (your accountant or tax adviser) or *a nominee* (another person). Write the account details in **Boxes 19.3** to **19.7**. If you want the refund to go to your accountant write that person's name in **Box 19.8** and their address in **Box 19.11**. If this person is your agent tick **Box 19.19** and write their reference for you in **Box 19.10**.

Note: **You must** sign **Box 19.12**. This is so your agent cannot ask for tax refunds to be sent to him or her without your consent.

Q20: CHECKING YOUR DETAILS

Are your details on the front of the Tax Return wrong? [NO] [YES]   If yes, please make any corrections on the front of the form.

Carefully check the details on the front of the Tax Return. If there are any errors, make your corrections on the front of the form.

Q21: PERSONAL DETAILS

Please give other personal details in boxes 21.1 to 21.6

Please give a daytime telephone number if convenient. It is often simpler to phone if we need to ask you about your Tax Return.

Your telephone number [21.1]
or, if you prefer, your agent's telephone number [21.2]
(also give your agent's name and reference in the 'Additional information' box on page 8)

165

Boxes 21.1 and 21.2:

It is very important that you fill in a daytime telephone number for either you or your tax adviser/accountant. If you give your agent's phone number write his or her name and reference in the 'Additional information' **Box** on page 8 of your Tax Return. By giving a telephone number you can often speed up the processing of your Tax Return and avoid lengthy correspondence with your Tax Office.

Boxes 21.3 and 21.6:

You must fill in your marital status.
Only fill in your date of birth if:

- ☐ you were born before 6 April 1933 (this is so you can claim higher age-related allowances);
- ☐ you are contributing to a personal pension or retirement annuity plan (you ticked the *YES* box in Question 14). This is because the amount you can contribute to a personal pension plan and receive tax relief on is dependent on age;
- ☐ you are claiming relief for venture capital trust subscriptions.

Q22: OTHER INFORMATION

Box 22.1: New pensions or benefits:

Tick this box if you expect to receive a new pension or Social Security benefit in the 1998/99 tax year. It will help your Tax Office to get your Tax Code right in the current tax year.

Box 22.2: Collection of tax:

Employees and those in receipt of company pensions or state benefits usually have small amounts of tax they owe collected through their Tax Code. This means that they do not have to pay a tax demand. However, the maximum that can be collected as additional tax in this way is £1000.

For example, if you are an employee and owe £600 in tax you can have this collected by an adjustment in the amount of tax you pay through PAYE. An additional £50 a month will be taken out of your

TAX REFUNDS, CALCULATIONS, OTHER INFORMATION

pay in tax, saving you from having to make a lump-sum payment.

Only tick this box if you do **not** want any taxed owed collected through your Tax Code. Note that if you tick the box and owe tax you will have to pay your outstanding tax as a lump sum – instead of over a year.

Box 22.3: Provisional figures:

In some cases you may not be able to get final or accurate figures but have to send back your Tax Return to meet the deadline. If this is the case you can use your best estimates.

Write in the 'Additional information' box which figures are provisional and what box numbers they relate to. You must state why you could not give the final figures and when you expect to get them.

But you must show that you have taken all reasonable steps to get this information. You cannot simply estimate vast amounts of your Tax Return because you have failed to file the relevant information or have not asked for it.

> **Tax tips:**
>
> ☐ Don't delay in sending back your Tax Return just because you are missing a couple of figures. If you miss the deadline for sending back your Tax Return you will be fined. Give the most accurate estimate you can, and then write to your Tax Office as soon as you have the final figures.
>
> ☐ You can amend or 'repair' your Tax Return within 12 months of sending it in. So, if you have made a mistake or have new information you can usually change your Tax Return without penalty (although you may have to pay interest on any outstanding tax that should have been paid earlier).

Box 22.4: rents paid overseas:

Rents paid overseas should have tax deducted at source (you or the landlord's agent must deduct tax before paying the rent to the overseas landlord), although in some cases you can pay rent without deducting tax if it is agreed by the non-resident landlord and the Inland Revenue. You need to tick this box to ensure that rents are taxed correctly. Do not forget to give the landlord's name and address in the 'Additional information' box.

FILLING IN YOUR TAX RETURN

Box 22.5: business losses and special rules for literary and artistic income:

This box will only apply if:

- ☐ you are self-employed or in partnership and want relief now for 1998/99 trading losses;
- ☐ have received income from a business that has ceased but want this taxed as income for an earlier year; or
- ☐ have literary or artistic income which you want to spread over two years or more.

If you tick this box do not forget to write the details in the 'Additional information' box.

THE 'ADDITIONAL INFORMATION' BOX

Make the most of this box. Read through the completed pages of your Tax Return to check if there is anything you want to – or need to – explain, question or bring to the attention of your Tax Office. Alternatively, if you are unsure about a particular box or question make a note of it here. Also make sure you have provided all the additional information that has been requested.

If you do not have enough room to include all these details you can write extra notes on an additional piece of paper and make a note of this enclosure in this box.

By providing this additional information, you may be able to prevent further investigation or correspondence from the Inland Revenue by answering any questions your Tax Inspector has.

Q23: DECLARATION

Check you have completed and enclosed all the supplementary pages and then tick the boxes in **Q23**.

Do not forget to sign the Tax Return. If a tax adviser or accountant is filling in the form for you, they can sign the form instead.

Remember to check your Tax Return carefully as once you have signed it you are legally responsible for its content.

Now photocopy all the pages and additional documents. If the

TAX REFUNDS, CALCULATIONS, OTHER INFORMATION

Inland revenue needs to contact you, you will need to have a record of what you have included on your Tax Return.

And finally... do not forget to pay your final tax bill by 31 January 1999. If you are calculating your own tax bill, you can send in a cheque with your completed Tax Return. If the Inland Revenue is calculating your tax bill, it will send you a demand.

18

CALCULATING YOUR TAX BILL

If you want to calculate your own tax bill – or have to because you missed the 30 September 1998 deadline for asking the Inland Revenue to do this for you – you should tick the *YES* box on page 7 of your Tax Return.

You should have received the green coloured Tax Calculation Guide (Form SA151) with your Tax Return.

But before completing it you should check that you do not need a different calculation guide.

You will need to request a different Tax Calculation Guide if you:

☐ have any chargeable gains (must pay Capital Gains Tax) – this will be the case if you have a figure in **Box 8.8** on the capital gains pages;
☐ have made any gains on UK and foreign life insurance policies – this will be the case if you have completed **Boxes 12.5** and/or **12.8**;
☐ have received lump sum and compensation payments and filled in **Box 1.29** on the Employment pages (or box 1M.45 if you are a minister of religion);
☐ received income from the estate of a deceased person with a notional basic-rate tax credit of 23 per cent – you will find this in **Box 7.18**;
☐ received a refund of surplus additional voluntary contributions from your pension scheme provider (see **Box 12.12**).

If you have filled in any of the boxes listed above you **must** request a different Tax Calculation Guide by ringing the Orderline on 0645 000 404 (open seven days a week between 8 am and 10 pm).

WARNING: Do **not** complete the Tax Calculation Guide until you have completed the main Tax Return and all the additional pages. Failure to complete all these forms will result in you miscalculating your tax.

CALCULTING YOUR TAX BILL

Note: Different rules apply for ministers of religion and Lloyd's underwriters who should take special care to read the notes on page 2 of the Tax Calculation Guide.

The Tax Calculation Guide is very complex so you should work through it with care. Remember that as you are self-employed you can deduct the cost of accountancy fees – so consider paying an accountant this rather than make a mistake in calculating your own tax liability.

19

A GUIDE TO THE OTHER SUPPLEMENTARY PAGES

The reason why the supplementary pages have been included at the end of this book (even though you should fill them in before completing the main eight pages of your Tax Return) is that they will not apply to everyone.

The employment and share scheme pages are not covered, as they only apply to employees not the self-employed.

LAND AND PROPERTY

These pages have to be filled in by anyone who received income from land and property in the tax year 6 April 1997 to 5 April 1998 – even if your rent is tax-free under the Rent a Room rules.

However, if you received income from renting out a holiday home **overseas** this should not be included here but on the Foreign pages.

If you received income from land and property that was owned in a partnership, that income should be included in the Partnership pages.

Land and property also includes rents from *immobile caravans* and permanent *houseboats*.

Under self-assessment you will have to make interim tax payments on account if 80 per cent or more of your rental income is untaxed and you owe more than £500 in tax.

PAPERWORK REQUIRED

It is essential for you to keep accurate and detailed records if you are to make the most of the expenses you can deduct from your

SUPPLEMENTARY PAGES: LAND AND PROPERTY

income to reduce your tax bill. These should include:

- ☐ rent, rates, insurance, ground rents, service charges, etc;
- ☐ any bills for repairs and maintenance;
- ☐ your mortgage interest statements or other loan details;
- ☐ any bills you have for legal, accountancy, surveying and other costs;
- ☐ details of any wages you have paid out.

WARNING: Before starting to fill in these pages make sure your accounts cover the same period as the tax year. If they do not, you will have to recalculate them so you only include income and expenses received and incurred during the tax year.

The rent a room scheme

This is the scheme that allows you to rent out a room in your home and receive up to £4250 a year – or £82 a week – tax free.

This only applies if the room is furnished, it is in your only or main home, and you do not run this as a business (such as a guest house).

You can only rent out **one** room and get the full £4250 allowance. You cannot try to claim two lots of allowance by getting someone else in your home to rent out a second room. If two rooms are let in the same property, one by you and one by someone you own the property with, the allowance is halved to £2125.

If you receive £4250 or less from renting out a room, tick the **YES** box on the top of the Capital Gains Tax page. There is no point in taking up the option of working out your profit as all of this rental income is tax free.

If you earn **more** than £4250 in rent you can *either* claim the Rent a Room allowance and pay tax on the amount of rent over this limit **or** be taxed on your rental profits. Your rental profits will be the amount you receive in rent minus the expenses. In most cases you will be better off claiming the rent-a-room allowance. Only work out the rental profits if your expenses are more than £4250. See below for a list of the type of expenses you can deduct.

> **Tax tip:** If your home is jointly owned, look at the tax advantages of splitting your Rent a Room Allowance if your rent exceeds the £4250 limit. If your spouse, or whoever else jointly owns your home, pays tax at a lower rate you will be better off splitting the rent so half of it is taxed at a lower rate.

FILLING IN YOUR TAX RETURN

Furnished holiday lettings

To qualify as furnished holiday lettings, the property must be:

- furnished;
- available for holiday letting to the public at a commercial rent for 140 days or more during the year; and
- actually let commercially as holiday accommodation for 70 days or more during the year; and
- not occupied continuously for more than 31 days by the same person for at least seven months of the year.

See page L2 of your tax notes for further details.

If you own and let holiday property with another or other people only include your share of rent and your share of expenses.

> **Tax tip**
>
> If your holiday letting nearly fits these criteria, make sure it does next year. There are tax advantages. For a start, if you make any losses you can use these to reduce your tax bill on earnings from employment or profits from self-employment. You cannot do this with other rental income – you can only use losses to offset against other property profits. Furnished holiday lettings have other tax advantages. You can claim capital allowances (a proportion of the amount you spend) on furniture, fixtures and fittings. With other types of rental income you can only claim for wear and tear of these items or the cost of replacing them. But you cannot claim capital allowances and replacement costs – only one or the other. Capital allowances are explained in Part 2, Chapter 9. You can also claim roll-over relief to defer your Capital Gains Tax liability if you sell one furnished holiday letting property and invest in another (see Chapter 2 on Capital Gains Tax).

You do not have to itemize expenses or fill in **Boxes 5.2** to **5.7** if your rental income is less than £15,000 a year. Just fill in the total amount claimed. A list of what can be deducted as expenses is included on page 179.

> **Tax tips:**
>
> - It may pay you to advertise or use an agency to attract tenants – not only is this a tax deductible expense but you can make sure you rent your property for at least 70 days a year so that your property qualifies as a furnished holiday letting.

SUPPLEMENTARY PAGES: LAND AND PROPERTY

> ☐ If you let more than one furnished holiday home you can average out the days the properties are let so you can pass the 70-day rule.

Box 5.10: private use

If you buy anything for your rented property that is also partly for private use you should put the **total** amount spent in the expenses **boxes** and then deduct the value of the proportion that was for private use here.

Boxes 5.16 to 5.18: losses

As discussed above furnished holiday lettings are the only type of rental you can use to offset losses against other income **and** capital gains. You can even use losses in this year **to reduce your tax bill in an earlier year**.

Also fill in **Box 5.19** overleaf but do not fill **Boxes 5.24** to **5.30** if you do not have any other income from rental property.

Other property income

This covers all property income other than furnished holiday lettings and the Rent a Room scheme (unless you want to opt out of this and be taxed on rental profits in the usual way). This broad category includes everything from leasing out acres of land to renting your property out to a film crew.

Do **not** include income from enterprise zone trusts. These go on page 3 of your main Tax Return.

Remember the rent is classed as being received when you earned it, **not** when you actually get paid. If you have a bad debt that you cannot reasonably recover you can deduct this.

And if you are paid in advance for rent and some of this relates to the period after 5 April 1997, this does not have to be included. You cannot evade tax by taking payment in kind – for instance you are given the free use of a car or other goods or services.

If your income is from the granting of a lease see page L5 of your notes for special rules.

Expenses

Don't itemize these if your total property income is less than £15,000 annually. But you will still need to know what are allowable expenses.

FILLING IN YOUR TAX RETURN

You cannot deduct the cost of buying the land or property or the cost of machinery, furnishings or furniture or any losses you make when you sell the land or property.

But you can deduct:

☐ any rent you pay to someone else for the use of the land or property;
☐ council tax, business rates, ground rents;
☐ heat and light (gas and electricity);
☐ insurance against loss of rent;
☐ insuring the property;
☐ maintenance and repairs from painting to roof repairs (but not a new roof) and damp course repairs (but not a new damp course);
☐ **interest on a loan to buy your property** and any costs incurred in arranging the loan;
☐ legal and professional costs of letting a property for a **year or less**;
☐ **accountancy fees for drawing up your accounts**;
☐ the costs of evicting a tenant;
☐ management expenses as a landlord – telephone calls, stationery, travelling for business purposes;
☐ advertising, estate agent and accommodation agency fees;
☐ **either** *wear and tear* – you cannot claim the purchase costs of equipment or furniture in a let residential property (unless it is a furnished holiday let) as an allowable expense. However you can claim 10 per cent for wear and tear of fixtures, fittings, cookers, even lampshades, beds and sheets. The figures are worked out using the rent you receive less service charges and water rates. You deduct 10 per cent of this figure to give your wear and tear allowance. So over ten years you should be able to recoup most of the initial costs;
☐ **or replacement and renewal** – this allows you to claim the full cost of replacing furniture, furnishings and household equipment – but only when you need to replace them.

Note: You have to choose between renewal expenses and wear and tear – you cannot have both and once you have chosen a basis you must stick to it. You cannot claim renewal expenses or wear and tear on items on which you have claimed a capital allowance.

You cannot claim for:
☐ the costs of your own time;

SUPPLEMENTARY PAGES: LAND AND PROPERTY

- ☐ the costs of buying the property (only loan interest);
- ☐ the costs of improving the property (this is deducted as a cost when you sell to reduce your Capital Gains Tax liability).

> **Tax tips:**
>
> ☐ If you are considering buying a home for letting you may be better off taking out a loan as interest payments are tax deductible and you do not have to tie up your capital.
>
> ☐ If it is your only or main home that you are renting out (say while you are working overseas) you may still be able to claim MIRAS – mortgage interest tax relief at source – which gives you 15 per cent tax relief on interest payments made on the first £30,000 of your home loan. Alternatively you can claim all the interest as an allowable expense and opt out of MIRAS. This will give you a bigger saving unless your rents are very low. Ask your Tax Office for advice.
>
> ☐ You can also claim wages paid to gardeners, porters, cleaners, etc. Consider employing your spouse if he or she is a non-taxpayer and does not earn enough to pay National Insurance (£3224 for 1997/98). This way you can pay the wage free of tax and save the hassle of calculating PAYE and National Insurance. But remember, work must actually be done.

Boxes 5.11 and 5.12 and 5.33 and 5.36:

Capital allowances enable you to tax deduct some of the purchase price of items you use in letting your property. **These cannot include furniture or household equipment unless the property is classed as a furnished holiday let.** However, if the property is not a furnished home (it is a commercial property) you can claim capital allowances on furniture, fixtures and fittings. All landlords can deduct the cost of any machinery or equipment used in maintaining the property such as ladders, tools and even garden equipment such as lawnmowers. You can also claim for the cost of constructing agricultural buildings, industrial and commercial buildings in enterprise zones and certain types of hotel.

If you sell the item for more than the written-down value (see Part 2, Chapter 9 on capital allowances chapter), include the amount you receive from the sale in **Box 5.11**. You will be taxed on this profit.

If you buy an item on hire purchase, you can claim capital allowances on the original cost of the item. The interest and other

FILLING IN YOUR TAX RETURN

charges are classed as expenses and should be deducted in **Boxes 5.4** and **5.26**.

If you opt for the renewal and replacement option you **cannot** claim for the initial purchase costs. So you cannot claim a capital allowance **and** for the cost of replacement on the same item.

> **Tax tip:**
>
> If an item that was previously for private use is now used in your business you can claim a capital allowance on its market value when you start using it for business.

If you only use items partly for business or want to know any more about capital allowances ask for *Help Sheet IR250*. If you want to claim agricultural buildings allowance ask for *Help Sheet IR224*.

Tax adjustments

As from 6 April 1995 all property you let is treated as one type of business and all income and expenses are aggregated (added up together) so you can offset one type of property loss against another (other than losses on overseas properties). Only losses from furnished holiday lets can be offset against other types of income (for instance income from employment or self-employment).

However, all rental losses can be *carried forward*. This means you can use your losses this year to reduce your profits from rental income in future years.

Agricultural estates or land managed as one estate are treated differently. Ask for *Help Sheet IR 251*.

> **Tax warning:**
>
> When you sell a property that has been let out you may have to pay capital gains tax on the profit. This will also be charged if you let part of your main home. See Chapter 2 on capital gains in Part I of this book.

FOREIGN INCOME

Do not confuse this with non-residence: 'foreign' covers income from overseas, whereas 'non-residence' is for those who live overseas.

This section covers savings that are in overseas or offshore

SUPPLEMENTARY PAGES: FOREIGN INCOME

accounts, dividends from overseas shares, offshore investment funds, overseas pensions and social security benefits and any income you receive from land and property including overseas holiday homes that you let out.

📄 PAPERWORK REQUIRED

You will need any dividend vouchers, bank statements, pensions advice notes, foreign tax assessments and receipts for foreign tax paid. If you invest in an overseas unit trust or investment fund you will need your fund voucher. If you have a property overseas you will also need to have all your receipts for expenses – from the cost of your mortgage to maintenance and caretaking bills. The guidance notes from the Inland Revenue (which you should ask for if you have not received them) are 22 pages long but only because each country has a different tax arrangement (or treaty) with the UK.

You will also need a calculator to help you convert all income into sterling.

These pages will enable you to reclaim any foreign Income Tax deducted on your overseas income. You can also reclaim Capital Gains Tax paid in a foreign country. You can use this to reduce (offset) some of your UK tax liability bill. You can calculate the tax credit yourself by following Part B in the notes provided by the Inland Revenue.

Note that this section does not deal with profits made on the sale of overseas homes or offshore and overseas shares and investments. You must include these on the Capital Gains pages.

> **Tax warning:**
> You will be taxed on your foreign income as you earn it, not on the date you bring the money into the UK or are paid it. However, if exchange controls mean you cannot bring the income into the UK it should not be taxable.

All amounts must be listed in sterling and you must use the exchange rate on the day you earned the foreign income (not received it or brought it into the UK). Working out what exchange rate to use can be difficult. Ask your Tax Office for help.

If you are resident in the UK but not domiciled here for tax purposes or are a citizen of the Commonwealth or the Republic of

FILLING IN YOUR TAX RETURN

Ireland special rules apply. These are the remittance basis rules and cover income you receive in the UK. Ask for the Non-residence pages by ringing the Orderline on 0645 000 404 and read the notes carefully.

If your savings and investments are in *joint names* enter only your share of the income.

> **Tax warning:**
> You can only reclaim foreign tax at the official rates agreed. There is a full list in your Inland Revenue guidance notes.

How to claim back foreign tax

If tax has been deducted from your foreign income by an overseas tax authority you can claim back the tax in one of two ways:

- by deducting it from the amount of income and gains which will be taxed in the UK (put this final figure in box E on the Tax Return); or
- by claiming tax credit relief. This is normally the best option. However, if the foreign tax is higher than the UK tax you can only claim *tax credit relief* up to the amount of UK tax you will pay. This tax credit will reduce your tax but only on the same income – it cannot be used to reduce tax on other types of income.

These rules ensure that you are not taxed twice. However, if you are not liable to UK income tax you cannot claim the extra foreign tax back by using the tax credit system.

If your foreign income is paid to you through a UK agent (eg a bank) tax will already be deducted. The agent should allow for any double taxation agreement.

Foreign savings

These include savings, interest and dividends but **not** offshore unit and investment trusts or other offshore funds.

Foreign income dividends (FIDS) from UK companies should be included on page 3 of your main Tax Return.

Each block of shares and each savings account is a separate source of income and should be listed separately. Shares bought at different times are also separate entries.

Ignore the unremittable box unless you are not domiciled in the UK for tax purposes but live in the UK **or** if you are a citizen of the Commonwealth or Republic of Ireland **and** are resident in the UK.

If you receive dividends from Finland, France, Italy or the Republic of Ireland you may be able to get the other country's tax credit in addition to any dividend. Add this tax credit to the dividend to get the figure to put in **Box B**.

> **Tax warning:**
>
> You cannot claim tax credit relief on dividends paid in some countries, including Cyprus, Malta, Jersey and the Isle of Man. But you can deduct the tax charged when calculating the amount of dividend on which you have to pay UK tax.

> **Tax tips:**
>
> ☐ If you hold savings accounts in joint names you can elect to have a larger share apportioned to the partner who pays tax at the lowest rate.
> ☐ You can get foreign tax reduced or claim another country's tax credit (for instance, tax on dividends), by writing to the Financial Intermediaries and Claims Office (International), Fitzroy House, PO Box 46, Nottingham, BG2 1BD, or by telephoning them on 0115-974 2000.

Overseas pensions and benefits

Some pensions and social security benefits are exempt from UK tax. Read page F7 of your Inland Revenue notes. Also note that only 90 per cent of the pension income from an overseas employer scheme or pension fund is taxed.

Remember if you are **not** claiming a foreign tax credit, deduct any foreign tax from your total pension or benefit (the figure in **Box B**) and write this figure in column E.

Income from land and property abroad

You must fill in the relevant section of page F2 (boxes A to E) **and** page F4. You will need a separate F4 for each property.

If, in a rare case, your rental income accounts are drawn up for a

FILLING IN YOUR TAX RETURN

year that is not the same as the tax year ask your Tax Office for advice. Only rent received or due in the tax year must be included on your Tax Return.

Read the land and property sections above for details of what you can deduct as expenses. Do **not** itemize expenses if your total income in the year before expenses is **less than £15,000**. If the property is leasehold you can claim for any rents you pay under the lease (or part of these rents if your home is only let out for part of the year). If you pay for caretakers and cleaners, overseas property agents and gardeners, claim for these along with advertising costs. You will find it difficult to claim the cost of air fares unless you can prove that the travel was *wholly and exclusively* for the purposes of the overseas letting business.

> **Tax tip:**
>
> You can deduct from your rental income interest you pay on You can deduct from your rental income interest you pay on a loan to buy the property abroad – (something that was not available before 6 April 1995).

You will need to fill a separate copy of page F4 for each property.

If you or your family use your overseas home for part of the year and rent it out for the remainder you must apportion your costs accordingly. The same applies if you only rent out part of the property.

Offshore funds

If you have invested in an offshore unit trust where income is automatically reinvested (roll-over funds) you still have to declare this income. The unit trust company should give you a tax voucher showing if foreign tax was deducted.

Some distributor funds have equalization arrangements, which means that part of your income may acually be a refund of capital. Check your redemption voucher. Any amount that is not a gain should be included in **Box 6.5**.

Foreign life insurance policies

Income and gains in most offshore insurance policies do not usually have foreign tax deducted but if it is deducted you **cannot** claim it as a tax credit relief and you **cannot** use it to reduce your gains in

Box 6.8. Life insurance policies are treated as though basic-rate tax is deducted. You only have to pay extra tax if you are a higher-rate taxpayer.

> **Tax tip:**
>
> Qualifying offshore life insurance polices do not give rise to taxable capital gains. These have to be a minimum of ten-year policies and must be approved by the Inland Revenue.

Foreign tax credits

Page F3 is for you to total up the tax credits you are claiming for foreign tax deducted on income in other sections of your Tax Return including:
- employment;
- self-employment;
- partnerships; or
- capital gains.

You can only claim tax credit relief if you have included the tax in the figures you have entered elsewhere. If you have deducted foreign tax before writing in your income, you cannot claim a tax credit as well.

TRUSTS

Trusts are a specialist area of tax. However, you do not have to know about trust law as the trust deed will have been drafted by a solicitor. You only have to know how much income you received from a trust. In this case you are the *beneficiary*.

You will also have to fill in this form if you are a *settlor*. This means you have set up a trust fund.

This section does not deal with unit or investment trusts. They should be included on your main Tax Return on page 3.

📄 PAPERWORK REQUIRED

All documentation given to you by the trustee of your trust. If you have received money from the estate of a deceased person you

FILLING IN YOUR TAX RETURN

should have a statement of the amounts paid from the estate by the personal representative who is administering the estate. All you have to do is copy this information onto the Trust page. If you are entitled to income from a trust by right (it is not a discretionary trust) you can ask your trustees for a certificate of income and tax deduction (Form R185E) which will detail the figures you need.

Before filling in the page you will need to know if the income you received is taxable and if it should be included on this page or another part of your Tax Return.

Income from trusts and settlements

The term *absolute right to income* means that you get that income automatically. It is not at the discretion of trustees. These include life interest trusts/interest in possession trusts. Because you have an automatic right to the income, for tax purposes the trust is disregarded. As such you must **not** include certain income on the Trusts page.

Include in section 10 of your main Tax Return:

- share dividends from UK companies;
- dividends from UK authorized unit trusts;
- dividends from investment trusts (open-ended investment companies).

Include on the Foreign pages:

- all foreign interest and dividends.

The representative administering the trust should tell you what to include on your Tax Return. Enter in **Box 7.3** the total gross income (without tax deducted), put the tax deducted (the amount of tax deducted at 23 per cent) in **Box 7.2** and the amount you actually received in **Box 7.1**.

If tax has been deducted at the lower 20 per cent rate (or you have a tax credit at that rate) fill in **Boxes 7.4** to **7.6**. Tax is deducted at the lower rate on share dividends and building society savings interest.

If there is *no absolute right to income* – for instance from a discretionary trust – you should have received all the information you need from the trustee, who should be able to tell you what types of income have been received on your behalf.

SUPPLEMENTARY PAGES: CAPITAL GAINS

Settlors

Those who set up trusts – may also have to declare their income in **Boxes 7.1** to **7.6**. This will be the case if you retain an interest in the trust. This simply means that the money could be paid to you in any circumstances whatsoever (however, remote the possibility). This could be from the beneficiary dying and the capital being returned to you or the trust deeds being written in such a way that you or your spouse could become beneficiaries.

You will also have to declare the income if you make a settlement in favour of children under 16 as any income that is paid to them is classed as being for your benefit. However, this will exclude gross (without tax deducted) income of £100 or less a year.

> **Tax tip:**
> To get round these rules you can get the grandparents to set up the trust.

Because these rules are so wide-ranging, if you are a settlor you should ask for *Help Sheet IR270* by ringing the Orderline on 0645 000 404.

Income from the estates of deceased persons

This does **not** include income earned on inheritances and legacies after they are paid to you. But while the estate is being managed and before you are paid any inheritance the estate may earn interest or rental income. This income is taxed in the relevant section of your Tax Return – for instance savings will be included on page 3 and property income in Land and property.

Fill in the relevant boxes:

- [ ] basic rate means 23 per cent tax has been deducted;
- [ ] lower rate means 20 per cent has been deducted – for instance from savings interest or share dividends;
- [ ] non-repayable – means tax has been deducted and you cannot reclaim this tax.

CAPITAL GAINS

Read the comprehensive guide to Capital Gains Tax in Part 1, Chapter 2 of this book for an explanation of what the tax is, who

FILLING IN YOUR TAX RETURN

pays it, what assets are covered and how to save tax.

You pay Capital Gains Tax if you sell or *dispose* of an *asset* – a possession, investment or business – and have made a *gain* or a profit. You pay the tax on the profit you make, **not** on the amount you receive when you sell the asset.

You are required to fill in the Capital Gains Tax pages if you have made profits (gains) on the sale of assets (investments, second homes, shares, antiques, inheritances) and:

- ☐ these total more than £13,000 (not each); or
- ☐ you have made profits of more than £6500;
- ☐ although the tax form does not stipulate this, you should also fill in the Capital Gains Tax pages if you made *losses* on the sale of assets. You can then use these to reduce your tax bill – either in this year, or in past or future years.

Even if you fall into one of these categories you may still not have to pay Capital Gains Tax. Some items are exempt and others will not be taxable because you can reduce your profits by deducting expenses and inflation (up until April 1998).

You will need a calculator as you have to do all the calculations yourself and will probably have to do them on a separate piece of paper. The actual form (once you have all the figures) is only two pages long.

📄 PAPERWORK REQUIRED

It is essential for you to keep accurate and detailed records in order to make sure you are filling in the right figures. You will have a major problem if you have not kept receipts or statements showing when you bought each item, how much you paid, any costs involved in the purchase and expenditure to improve the item, and how much you sold it for.

Filling in your capital gains tax form

Page CG2:

It is important that you give as much information as possible so that the Tax Office does not have to make further enquiries. If there is not enough space, photocopy the form, ask for an additional Capital

SUPPLEMENTARY PAGES: NON-RESIDENCE

Gains Tax page or send a covering letter with your Tax Return.

Include details like the address of the building or description of the property you sold, the name of the company in which you held shares, or the address and type of business you sold.

And in the further information box explain your figures, what reliefs have been claimed, if you have only sold part of the asset, etc.

Column 7 should be ticked if you want to claim relief from Capital Gains Tax. For instance, if you want roll-over relief tick this box and explain the type of relief in column 8.

Once you have totalled up the figures on page CG2 they only need to be copied into the boxes on CG1.

Boxes 8.1 to 8.7: Chargeable gains and allowable losses

In the first box write your total chargeable gains (if there is more than one item you will have to add these up) and in the second any losses. Subtract losses from gains to fill in either **Box 8.3** or **8.4** depending on if you made a net gain or loss.

If the figure in **Box 8.3** is less than £6500 (the Capital Gains Tax allowance) you will not have to pay any Capital Gains Tax so ignore the rest of these boxes and move to **Box 8.10**.

In **Box 8.5** you use any trading losses from your business to reduce your Capital Gains Tax liability. You can also offset post cession expenditure and losses from furnished holiday lettings.

WARNING: If you offset losses to reduce your capital gains to less than £6500 (the Capital Gains Tax threshold) you will lose some of your tax free allowance. Whenever possible, try not to reduce gains to below £6500.

Any losses from previous tax years you have not used to reduce past capital gains, can be used to offset capital gains in this tax year. Write the amount in **Box 8.6** and once again do not reduce your chargeable gains to less than £6500. If you use up all your past losses, you can then write 'O' in **Box 8.20** and **8.21**.

If you have sufficient losses to reduce your gains to £6500 in **Box 8.6** write the amount that, combined with any figure in **Box 8.5**, will reduce your gains to £6500 exactly.

Follow the instructions in **Box 8.7** to calculate your chargeable gains and then in **Box 8.8** deduct your tax allowance of £6500. This will give you your taxable chargeable gains for 1997/98.

Boxes 8.10 to 8.17: Capital losses

These boxes need to be filled in so you can keep track of your allowable losses from past years and this year. This is information you will need when filling in next year's Tax Return.
Note: If you have filled in the Capital Gains Tax pages, you will need to fill in a different Tax Calculation Guide SA152 if you are planning to calculate your own tax.

NON-RESIDENCE

There are major tax advantages to being taxed elsewhere – in a tax haven or country with much lower tax rates than the UK – and as such the Inland Revenue keeps a careful watch for abuse of the rules.

There are different tax treatments depending on whether you are not resident, not domiciled or not ordinarily resident in the UK.

As such all the questions on the two pages covering non-residence are about you, your nationality and the amount of time you spend in the UK. No income figures have to be filled in.

Until the recent budget if you earnt money overseas you were taxed on it in the UK unless you were absent from the UK for an entire tax year. However, this tax break did not extend to the self-employed and only applied to employees. See pages NR9 to NR13 of your Inland Revenue guidance notes for what is taxable and what is not under each tax status. However, the March 1998 budget tightened the rules, making it even harder to avoid paying tax in the UK.

Because each question on the Non-residence pages is straightforward and relates to your individual circumstances there is little point in telling you how to fill in the 47 different Boxes. However, it will be useful for you to know how your answers will affect the way you are taxed.

The definition of non-residence

The term non-resident generally refers to those who spend less than 183 days in the UK in any tax year and less than 91 days a year over a four-year average (for this Tax Return that will be since 5 April 1994).

The advantage of being a non-resident was that you pay UK Income Tax **only** on your UK earnings and **not** on your worldwide

SUPPLEMENTARY PAGES: NON-RESIDENCE

income.

But remember you will have to pay tax in the country where you are living. If the taxes are higher in that country than in the UK you may be better off spending more days a year in the UK and being taxed at UK tax rates. If the tax rates are lower, spend fewer days in the UK.

If you were not 'present' in the UK during the tax year, you are a non-resident (however, that does not mean you cannot be ordinarily resident). You can be non-resident on a yearly basis – this status does not have to be permanent.

However, if you are in the armed forces or diplomatic service or another Crown employee you will be taxed as if you worked in the UK. However, any extra allowance paid for working abroad is not taxable.

If you have only recently left the UK (since 6 April 1997) and were ordinarily resident in the last tax year ending 5 April 1997 you **cannot** claim to be a non-resident.

Only if you have:

- [ ] spent the last tax year abroad (you left the UK before 6 April 1997);
- [ ] are working full-time in another country;
- [ ] have settled in another country and made it your home; or
- [ ] are intending to live in that country for another three years.

Can you now claim to be **non-resident** if you meet the rules of spending fewer than 183 days in the UK in any one tax year or visiting the UK for fewer than 91 days a year over a four-year average.

You will count as non-resident from the day after you leave until the day before you come back to live in the UK.

The reason why the Tax Return asks for your nationality is that certain long-term UK residents are still regarded as UK residents even if they leave the UK for occasional residence abroad. These include Commonwealth citizens, British citizens and EEA nationals. So you may have to prove that your departure is more than temporary – usually three years or more – and that you have established a home overseas unless you have spent a complete tax year overseas. Also these non-residents can still continue to claim UK personal tax allowance against any income subject to UK tax.

You can be resident in the UK at the same time as being resident

FILLING IN YOUR TAX RETURN

in another country. In this case you will have to make sure you are not taxed twice.

> **Tax tips:**
> - ☐ The rules covering residency relate to entire tax years but if you arrive or leave the UK part way through a tax year you should still be able to claim full UK personal allowances (the amount you can earn before paying tax).
> - ☐ If you are working overseas and are classed as a non-resident but your wife/husband is still resident in the UK, you can transfer unused married couple's allowance to the UK resident.
> - ☐ If you work overseas for 365 days or more you can no longer claim the foreign earnings deduction which means all your earnings from employment overseas are no longer free of UK tax. There is a box on your Employment pages for you to claim this. You can still visit the UK but not for more than a sixth or 62 days of the 365 days.
> - ☐ If you are a non-resident transfer investments overseas to an offshore tax haven so that income can be earned free of UK tax. And apply for your bank and building society interest to be paid gross (without tax deducted).
> - ☐ If you do have investments here, under the double tax treaties with many other countries you can apply for double tax treaty relief.
> - ☐ If you are non-resident in the UK make the most of this tax status.

Different rules apply to those coming to live in the UK. They will be treated as **resident** in the UK for tax purposes if they came to live here before the end of the tax year and either intended to live here for two years or more or have already lived here for more than two years. If you came to the UK before 6 April 1997 and have intended to remain in the UK for more than two years you are also resident in the UK. If you came to live in the UK before 6 April 1993 and have spent more than 363 days here in the four years ending 5 April 1997 or have arrived here in the last tax year and intend to spend more than an average 91 days a year over a four-year period here, you will also be resident for tax purposes in the UK.

The definition of ordinary residence

This is a little more permanent than the residence status. Ordinary residence applies to those who intend to make – or have made –

their home abroad, so this will not usually change from year to year.

Those coming to the UK to live will be classed as ordinarily resident if they spend 91 days a year or more on average over four years in the UK. However, if it is intended that this will be the case ordinary residence can be established from the outset.

If your home is here and you are usually resident in the UK and have been for the last four years, you are ordinarily resident here. To qualify as ordinarily resident elsewhere you must generally be resident there for four years. If you apply for a residency permit and have a home overseas and show that you intend to make another country your home, you can also be classed as ordinarily resident overseas.

The same tax rules apply as for non-residence.

The definition of domicile

This implies even more permanence. Becoming domiciled in another country – particularly one with lower tax rates than the UK – can have its advantages. Generally you will have to buy a property in your new country, make a will under its law, apply for permanent residence (if not nationality), dispose of your UK residence, close UK bank accounts and open ones in your new country. So you have to take major steps to prove that you are a permanent resident in your new country and show that there is no intention to return to live in the UK.

That is why your domicile is normally regarded as your homeland and the country where you intend to die. Again you are allowed to visit the UK for up to 90 days a year.

If you are domiciled outside the UK you should be taxed on your worldwide income at the tax rate in your new country. However, UK earnings will still be taxed in the UK.

If you come to live in the UK you will be required to fill in a domicile questionnaire (DOM1) to ascertain your domicile.